MISHAP
IN
MILSAP

A TIMELY MESSAGE
FOR THE USA

JOSEPH M. WOLFE

LUCIDBOOKS

Mishap in Milsap
A Timely Message for the USA

eISBN: 978-1-63296-432-8
ISBN: 978-1-63296-431-1

To my young bride, Lynelle, the Queen of Wolfetopia, for your enduring patience and endeavoring spirit, for your faithfulness in turmoil and perseverance in trials, for your passion for education and your fellowship on the journey, for your godliness, goodness, and generosity

TABLE OF CONTENTS

Chapter 1	1
Chapter 2	5
Chapter 3	13
Chapter 4	19
Chapter 5	23
Chapter 6	27
Chapter 7	31
Chapter 8	39
Chapter 9	43
Chapter 10	49
Chapter 11	57
Chapter 12	63
Chapter 13	69
Chapter 14	77
Chapter 15	81
Chapter 16	87
Chapter 17	95
Chapter 18	99
Chapter 19	105
Chapter 20	113
Chapter 21	117
Chapter 22	119
Chapter 23	125

Chapter 24   129

Chapter 25   133

Chapter 26   137

Chapter 27   139

Afterword   141

Appendix 1: Jwo's Blog   143

Appendix 2: One More Goodbye   157

CHAPTER 1

The first thing she heard when she arrived was a muted song with this lyrical chant:

> Emergency, emergency
> You live your life in urgency, urgency
> 'cuz crisis is the currency you trade in.

She slowly turned around and took in her surroundings. It was not a spectacular site, and it was unfamiliar to her. As she took in the scenery, a small crowd encircled her. She noted that they didn't seem like the friendly type, and they appeared to mean her harm. Their coordinated blue attire led her to believe that they were a band or a tribal unit coming to protect their territory that, unbeknownst to her, she had suddenly invaded. They carried clubs, sticks, and shiny objects. She waited patiently for the leader to speak up. Finally, a tall, dark-colored man demanded, "What is your business here?"

Interesting, she thought, as she wondered about the type of business that had brought her to this place in time. *More importantly,* she thought, *how can I explain this "business"?*

Having settled on a direct approach, she responded, "I bring a message of the future for your people."

The leader took off his blue cap and sighed. "What type of message could possibly be so important that you would break into Police Headquarters to deliver it?"

In an interview room, across the table from one of the subordinate tribe members known as the Police, she answered question after question—some regarding identification, her method of entry, the message she was carrying.

"And I shall repeat, I do not have an A dress. I only have what you see here. I did not break into this building; I am merely here," she was saying.

"Okay, Leonab, assuming that is your real name. How did you get here?" replied the subordinate.

"That is of less import than *why* I am here."

"Okay, then tell me *why* you are here. What is this message for our people? Is it for the Police Department specifically?"

"It is a message of hope for the future, but it requires a drastic change. These changes are critical for the future of your people and mine."

"Okay, and who are your people?"

Just then the door contraption opened, and someone motioned the subordinate to exit the room. As the door closed behind him, Leonab thought on his last question: *Who are my people?* She had recently learned English, but the dialect her present captors spoke seemed less refined somehow. *How can I explain?* She had time to ponder this question; life had taught her to be patient. As she sat, she thought about her family and all she had left behind in pursuit of this mission. Why had she been chosen for a task of this magnitude? Had Yala known she would face these obstacles? What are Fanto and Bontaq doing? She realized this was a silly question since they didn't exist in this time. Still, she couldn't help but think of them. While she understood the illogical nature of the inquiry, she could not compel her subconscious to dismiss on command; otherwise, it would be conscious. She had learned that with significant self-discipline, training, and practice, one could influence one's own subconscious tendencies, but her travels and experience had taught her that this was a long-term process. While Yala had planned this mission long before her, she had not had sufficient time or understanding to have prepared for this time-space paradox. *After all*, she thought, *how do we interact with others without understanding our identity in and relation to our own families?*

When the door opened again, the leader entered. "My name is Richard Crondell," he said. "I'm the Police Chief here in Milsap. Now, Leonab, is it?"

"Yes, sir," she responded.

"You gave us quite a scare popping in here like that. No one saw you enter or pass through our security, and somehow you evaded our security cameras altogether. I don't know how you accomplished this last feat since it is a physical impossibility. But, as you apparently pose no harm and have no nefarious intentions, you are free to go." The Police Chief opened the door to the interrogation room.

"Do you mean to say that I am under suspicion of something?" Leonab asked.

"Not anymore. As I said, you are free to go," responded the Police Chief.

"But what about my message for your people?" persisted Leonab.

"Look, lady, I'm not a counselor . . . What I mean is that you need to seek a different institution for the kind of help you, um, are requesting." As he ushered her to the front door of the building, he grabbed a city map off the information counter and handed it to her. "You see the red circle with a white plus sign in the middle? That's the hospital where you should go to deliver your message. I'm sure you'll find what you need there. This"—he indicated the box marked MPHQ—"is where we are now."

CHAPTER 2

Stew hadn't gotten enough sleep, as was his usual Thursday routine. He probably should have been at home helping with chores around the house, but when he'd woken up this afternoon, he'd snuck out of the house undetected. On occasion, he would drive to the school, theater, or church and walk around to think through his life circumstances. Today, he had chosen to do his soul-searching downtown.

I wonder if I should move away from home, he thought, *get a fresh start.* He considered his parents and the values they had taught him growing up. He thought about his job and the pressure he felt looking death in the face every other day. *If there is a God, why do all these bad things happen? Do they happen in every town or just in ours? That's kind of silly. Surely, if they happen here, they happen everywhere. The national news makes it seem like the rest of the country is an open penitentiary. Maybe I should just stay here.* As he walked, he saw yet another sign advertising the upcoming mayoral election debate. *This town has a small-town feel, but it has big-town problems, that's for sure.*

Stew thought about the growing conflicts among the people in Milsap, but the problems were particularly close to him as he faced them daily at home. While he tried to live by the values he'd been taught, they seemed to be conditional, even optional at times. *I just can't quite put my finger on what, how, or maybe why. I don't even know what the question is. Maybe I'm just facing a midlife crisis.*

As Leonab exited the building, she noted its dull color and plain, grainy texture. She looked around and saw numerous similar structures of varying shades and sizes. *Is this a representation of my people? What is to become of them?* She had a potential answer from the mission she was on, but that was a scary thought. *How can I communicate the message to help them secure their future?* she questioned. Then she remembered, *I'm not exactly sure what the message is. Perhaps the people at the white plus sign in the red circle will know.*

She opened the map and traced her finger down the drawn paths from the box marked MPHQ to the red circle marked with a white plus sign. As she stepped onto what she presumed to be the path, a large, self-propelled contraption nearly flattened her before she jumped aside.

A kindly, young gentleman ran to help her up from where she'd fallen. "Are you okay?"

Leonab started but accepted the proffered hand. "I thank you, kind sir, for your concern," she said.

"Well, you have to look both ways before crossing the street. Didn't your momma ever teach you that?" the gentleman responded. He smiled a sincere, dimpled smile.

"Oh, I'm not from here," she replied.

"And where are you from?" he inquired.

As she thought of how to respond to this question, she thought, *A better question would have been, "From when are you?"* But thankfully, he hadn't asked that. She politely responded, "That is a long story, and I should be on my way."

"Where are you headed? Maybe I can escort you there to keep you out of trouble," he responded.

"That is very kind. I am going to this white plus sign on the red circle," she replied, indicating the location on the map. "Do you know how to get there?"

"You're going to the hospital? I work there, so sure, I know where it is. Are you some kind of a doctor or something?" he asked doubtfully.

"I don't think so," she responded. "I am on my way to deliver a message to your people."

"Oh. What type of message?"

"A message about the future."

"Oh, I see," he said with raised eyebrows. "Well, I can definitely help you get there."

The kindly stranger escorted Leonab to his own contraption and opened the door for her. She got in, and he walked to the other side and opened another door. She noticed that this particular enclosed contraption apparently had four doors, and she thought how inefficient that seemed given the relatively small space within. *So many openings and closings for such a small space. Interesting.*

Leonab introduced herself and then learned that the man's name was Edward, but most people called him Stew. He continued making conversation. "I was born in Milsap 37 years ago, and I've been here ever since. I live with my mom and dad just up the road. My parents are ministers at a local church here in Milsap. Would you like to meet them?"

Leonab thought about the importance of her message and the lack of content of that message. Her thoughts then turned to her own home and family. She reflected on the earlier mishap of her arrival and decided she should observe more of this culture, the people, and the customs to clarify what the message was to be. "Okay, I will accompany you."

As they drove, Stew told Leonab how he had gotten his nickname. "Most guys named Edward are called Ed, and those named Steward are called Stew. But my parents didn't want me to be called Ed . . . "

Leonab was listening, but she was distracted by the mission she was on. *His parents insisted on calling him Edward instead of Ed . . . something to do with a talking horse.* At this, she decided to pay attention to what he was saying in case she ran into talking horses.

"Then, when my formal education began in elementary school, I had a tendency to get into hot water," he said.

Leonab thought about how odd it was to call primary education "elementary" since it consisted of the fundamental years of learning when the most important lessons of life were taught. It seemed ridiculous to label these lessons basic or simple. Lessons learned in the formative years of one's life were not elementary at all but of primary import.

As she was distracted thinking of this, Stew rambled on about some mischievous event when he had upset the school cook, something to do with the cooking pot having hot water for stew. She wasn't exactly sure if this was the hot water that Stew had gotten into, if he'd spilled the stew, or if he'd put some foreign floating object in the stew, but she laughed politely when he finished. *That trivial detail will likely not be significant*, she thought.

The self-propelled contraption, she noted, was similar to a horse-drawn encased carriage. It also required a conductor to guide it with a circular device that protruded immediately in front of Stew. *Is this some kind of a horse? Does this horse talk?* she wondered. He had first depressed some button, apparently to wake the beast. By the time Stew finished laughing, they had stopped, and he was opening his door. As Leonab was unprepared for their immediate arrival, she failed to observe how the door-opening mechanism was activated. She waited patiently until he noticed her failure to exit and proceeded to open the door for her. He showed her how the door latch worked. "They're different on every car," he said.

She noticed that the door handle was in the middle of the door, which seemed so inefficient. *Handles should be close to the openings*, she thought. She looked up at what Stew had indicated as his parents' house. It was a reasonably large structure, not as large as Police Headquarters, but it also had seemingly transparent square holes on either side of the principal door. *Strange*, she thought. *This society apparently invites onlookers to peer into the privacy of the very souls of their families.* Once inside, she began noticing all sorts of odd and seemingly unnecessary things.

When Stew touched the wall, some artificial light appeared. Leonab noted that a central candlestick hanging upside down from the ceiling in the room was the source of the light. There were no openings there. *Do all rooms in this time have their own artificial suns?* she thought. *Was there one like this at the Police Headquarters in the room where I was questioned?* She was sure that the enclosed building had no candles.

There were rectangles of colored images on the walls, some in various likenesses, others apparently random in nature. There were soft-looking seats, and only the most prominent rectangular image was in plain view from every seat except one chair in a corner near it. The image on the screen, however, was blank. *Perhaps these people are not as lost as I initially presumed,* she thought. *The presence of the blankness in such a prominent position must signify a culture that often reflects on those who have gone before, perhaps even those represented by the images in the other rectangles in the room. Or maybe in the blankness of this rectangle, they focus on the emptiness of their own souls or look to the future as a blank slate to be written by their own actions and choices they will make.*

Stew, noting that Leonab was staring at the TV, grabbed the remote and turned the TV on. "Is there something you want to watch?" he asked.

All of a sudden, there was a cacophony of noise and chaos coming from the previously blank screen. Leonab started. "What is that?"

Stew muted the TV and said, "Oh, I asked if you want to watch something on the TV," as he gestured to the magic rectangle. "We have Netflix, so you can watch anything you want."

Leonab was taken aback but quickly regained her composure. "Oh, I thank you, but no. I was just peering into the blankness considering the serenity of the emptiness that stands in sharp contrast to the busyness that surrounds us."

"Okaaay," Stew said as he turned the TV off.

"Stew, honey, is that you, dear?" came a call through the house.

"C'mon," Stew said, "you can meet my folks."

Leonab thought to herself, *Is "c'mon" a complete sentence in this time?*

"Yeah, Mom. It's me. I brought home a new friend." Stew led Leonab through to the back of the house where she encountered a large table with several seats around it. She noticed at the other end of the room, which also had artificial lights hanging from the ceiling, a door that appeared to have no handle, but as she was observing this, it opened toward them, and a graying lady appeared.

"Mom, this is Leonab," Stew said. "Leonab, this is my mom, Sister Gofson."

"If she is your mother, why then do you call her your sister?" asked Leonab inquisitively.

"Oh, I don't call her that. Other people do. I call her Mom," Stew replied as if having been chided.

"Are these other people your siblings, then?" Leonab asked the lady.

"No, dear. It's just a formality. You may call me Mrs. Gofson if you prefer," she replied. She motioned to the kitchen and said, "Stew, a word."

Leonab thought again, *Language use in this time is so strange. That sentence—"A word"—had no predicate at all.* She watched as Stew followed Mrs. Gofson through the door with no handles. She assumed they were talking since at the very least she considered it a safe conclusion that "a word" indicated actual dialogue, with or without subjects and verbs. She, being the polite lady she had been raised to be, amused herself patiently. She had come to this house to observe and not criticize.

"This is the fourth stray you have brought here this year, Stew. How long is this one going to stay?" Stew's mom asked him.

"She stumbled out of Police Headquarters into the street on her way to the hospital, Mom. I just brought her here to meet you and Dad. I'll take her to the hospital tomorrow when I go in for my shift," Stew responded.

"Well, she'll have to share the room with Diana and Lily because we don't have another bedroom available in the house. What about them and their friend Billy? When are those strays going to move on? What am I going to do with you, son? We don't have room and food for all these vagabond freeloaders you bring home all the time," Mrs. Gofson said.

"The hospital can't help those people, just as the police couldn't help Leonab. I know that not everyone appreciates our help, but we are still called to be generous, right? Didn't you teach me that?" Stew countered.

Mrs. Gofson hesitated and then finally relented. "I'll go up and see about accommodating Leonab with Diana and Lily. You'd better get her things from the car."

"Uh, she didn't have any things," Stew said awkwardly.

"Oh," Mrs. Gofson replied. "That's odd."

CHAPTER 3

Mrs. Gofson accompanied Leonab upstairs to meet the other girls living there. They were about the same age as Leonab and were peering at what looked like a smaller, handheld version of the TV. After short introductions and instructions about dinner being at some numeric time reference, Mrs. Gofson left the girls alone.

"So, Leonab, if that is your real name, what do you think of Jwo's latest blog?" the girl named Diana asked.

"Leonab is my real name. Who is Jwo, and what is a blog?"

"He's only the greatest philosopher who ever lived," answered Diana. "Everybody's talking about him."

"No, they are not," responded Lily sharply. "He is only some no-name hothead who is spouting philosophy like poetry through digital means. He's no Aristotle. We don't even know how to properly pronounce his name. Is it Jew-o or Jew-oo, or Jay-wo, or Jay-woo, or some other weird permutation?"

"What, pray tell, does he say?" asked Leonab.

"Get a load of this," Lily said as she began reading.

A more appropriate interpretation of these imperfections is that they validate the clear distinction between history and History as defined in another work; fundamentally that history is from the subjective perspective of the observer and is imperfect but knowable while History is objective from outside all observers and perfect but unknowable to the observers.

The author is hesitant to differentiate the future from the Future. The author does not wish to imply that the Future is established as History is; however, it is convenient to distinguish an individual's projections of potential future events versus what actually will happen in the Future.

Events of the Future are similar to Historical events in that an individual may know that some event has occurred in History or an event will occur in the Future, but the precise details cannot be fully comprehended. For instance, each individual was born in his/her own past, yet the details cannot be fully known in the Past; and each individual will someday die in their future, though we cannot be certain of the time, place, or circumstances in the Future.

"Just for clarity, Jwo also explains, with significantly more words than necessary, as any intellectual will, that the past, lowercase *p*, and the Past, uppercase *P*, are also relative and absolute, respectively," she added. "So, is that a load of crock or what?"

"Seems consistent with my understanding and experiences," Leonab said.

Diana chuckled. "See, Lily? Jwo is pure genius."

Lily responded dubiously to Leonab, "Your experience? And what, pray tell, is your experience? Where are you from, anyway? What kind of name is Leonab, anyhow? It's like Leona with a *b* tacked on at the end."

Leonab saw a somewhat safe environment to acquire a bit of cultural insight from these two girls, but she determined to tread carefully. "In my homeland, we are not accustomed to many of your society's peculiarities. For instance, the small teevees you are reading. What is their purpose?"

Lily stared at Leonab for a few seconds, incredulous. "You've seriously never seen a cell phone?" she demanded. "Your experience, whatever. This is not a TV; it's called a cell phone. We use it to, you know, talk to people who are far away or send messages to individuals or groups of people. We were just reading the random thoughts of Diana's great prophet, Jwo."

"And do other prophets communicate this way?" Leonab asked.

"Girl, just about anyone can communicate whatever message they want this way. Let me show you." With a few taps of her fingertips on her cell phone, Diana showed Leonab her screen, which read, "Moon landing: science or conspiracy?" "See?" she said. "There are people who present all kinds of crazy arguments on either side of any contentious or noncontentious event. All sides have the freedom to post whatever they want, and whoever wants to read it can."

"Look, here's a video explaining how God created the world in seven days, like these preacher-types Mr. and Mrs. Gofson tell us about. And here's another video explaining that the cosmos is all there ever was," Lily said.

15

Leonab looked confused. She thought about the moon and the cosmos, but she couldn't get distracted with specific details. "And how many of these prophets and messages are there?" she asked.

"Seems like these days, everyone's a digital prophet. Okay, well that's not exactly true. Most people only post info about what they are eating or what great adventure they are on, or maybe how miserable their lives are. But anyone can create a cause and present an argument for or against it," Diana responded.

"So how do the rest of your people learn of these causes?" Leonab asked with interest.

"Well, unless you are really famous or become really famous, people have to basically stumble over your blog," answered Lily.

"That seems like an ineffective way to communicate any urgent message en masse. What about this prophet Jwo? He sounds well educated. Is he famous?" Leonab followed up.

"No," lamented Diana. "He only has a few followers."

"Yeah," added Lily, "I think Diana accounts for three of his 12 followers."

"Get a life, Lily," quipped Diana.

Lily responded, "Diana, you have got to grow up. No one is going to come and sweep you off your feet and rescue you from your pathetic life. Stew's kindness will only carry us so far. At some point, we will have to pick up and move on."

"Will you share with me the most important of the messages from the digital prophets?" Leonab interjected.

Stifling a sob, Diana answered, "We don't need blogs and prophets to identify the most important issues of the day, but you do have to know what side of the issues you're on to decide whether or not they are important to you. Are you pro or con, for or against?"

Confused, Leonab said, "Wait! Are you saying that before one can make a determination as to what topic is of utmost import, they must first determine what stance to take on said topic?"

"Pretty much," said Lily. "But perhaps we are just cynics. Now Diogenes—there was a philosopher."

"Well, since you clearly aren't from around here," said Diana with a contemptuous look toward Lily, "perhaps we could explain some of the key topics from both sides and let you decide how they all fit together."

Lily smiled at Diana. "But we'd better do that later. It's 6:00, dinnertime."

CHAPTER 4

As the girls walked out of the bedroom into the larger meeting room between two upstairs bedrooms, the boys, Stew and Billy, were already heading down the stairs. Stew, hearing the door open, looked up and waved. Diana and Leonab waved back, but Lily did not. At dinner, Leonab was introduced to Billy and to Brother—or Mr.—Gofson.

Mrs. Gofson served small portions of roast, green beans, and mashed potatoes. All of it seemed very inefficient to Leonab, each person with his or her own saucer for food with hand utensils and three separate dishes for serving. Although she hadn't observed any other evidence of an exit from the room behind the door with no handles, she assumed there must be one because the food was hot, and surely no one would light a fire inside the house.

Leonab was careful to observe and imitate the behavior of Diana, who sat across from her. As they ate, Mr. Gofson attempted polite conversation. "So, Leonab, is it? That's a unique name. What is your ancestry?" Everyone looked interested to hear her answer.

"Well," she said, "that is a complicated question. When I was young, my family moved from place to place, so I don't really have a place of origin. But I'm here now."

"Are you a Native American? I bet so from your skin tone." Billy opened his mouth for the first time.

"Billy!" exclaimed an abashed-looking Mrs. Gofson. "Mind your manners."

"Very interesting, indeed," said Mr. Gofson. "So does your family keep many of their native customs? I mean, you speak English like you grew up speaking it. Do you also speak your native tongue?"

"Oh, we speak our own native tongue, and I have studied English with all my traveling," answered Leonab. "We also have our own customs. For instance, in my home, we, too, have an object similar to your teevee, only it does not show moving scenery or emit sounds. It is a blank emptiness. After we eat the evening meal, we sit together around the teevee and peer into it, reflecting on the darkness of our souls. We think of the ones we have lost— our mothers, sisters, fathers, brothers, children, husbands, wives, friends. This reflection is experienced collectively, but it is lonely. It is somber and sacred. If ever you were to see one sitting and gazing into the teevee alone, you should join him or her because deep loneliness is heavy and not meant to be experienced by oneself."

"That's a contradiction," interrupted Mr. Gofson. "I mean, by definition, loneliness means, well, being alone."

"Indeed," answered Leonab, "but loneliness is not meant to be a state of being. It is an emotion, a feeling. We are not made to be alone. Even the Great Y—" She caught herself. "—the Great One said, 'It is not good for them to be alone.'"

"So, you are familiar with the Bible? That's excellent," reflected Mr. Gofson.

As he was about to pursue some spiritual continuation, Diana interrupted. "So your TVs communicate sadness? That seems depressing."

"No," responded Leonab. "That's not the end; it's just the beginning. We do reflect upon our own emptiness, the loss of our family and friends. But just when the loneliness is ready to consume us individually, one person or another is compelled internally and spontaneously to speak words to music—sometimes more than one person at a time. These words embrace the loneliness of loss we feel and then honor those who have gone before, and ultimately, they culminate in a proclamation of the future reunion we shall have. It is the emptiness of the teevee that demonstrates our own futility, but it is in that same emptiness that we are able to set aside all our distractions and busyness to focus on what is really important."

"And what exactly is that?" Lily sounded skeptical.

Stew spoke up. "Lily, have you not seen in this house that life is about serving and loving others? It sounds like that is exactly what Leonab is telling us. Remember that passage of scripture that Jwo referenced in last week's post? 'Jesus . . . for the joy that was set before him endured the cross.' He saw through the loneliness of the cross and the emptiness of humankind and was willing to sacrifice himself for our sakes. Perhaps Jesus had been gazing into Leonab's TV."

"Interesting conjecture, Stew," commented Mr. Gofson, "but Jesus wasn't Native American. Still, you are right that Leonab's culture seems acutely aware of the principles of Christianity."

"What is Christianity?" asked Leonab innocently.

"Here we go," sighed Lily.

Mrs. Gofson cleared her throat. "Suffice it to say, it is our system of beliefs and our guide to how we live life based on a promise made by God, perhaps your Great One, and the life and sacrifice of his Son, Jesus Christ. Stew says you need to get to the hospital. Perhaps you can stay here for a few weeks as you see to your, ahem, business there. You can learn about Christianity while you are here." Stew smiled at his mother.

CHAPTER 5

Having ended dinner, Mr. and Mrs. Gofson instructed the boys and girls on cleanup duties. Lily took charge once the couple was out of the way. Working together, they quickly washed, dried, and put away the dishes. This was Leonab's first view of the room behind the door with no handles. As she had deduced, there was, indeed, a door leading to the outside. Lily handed her a towel and put her in charge of drying the dishes.

It was the first efficient process Leonab had witnessed in her new setting. Diana cleared the table and put away extra food in a large, freestanding box with two doors that seemed to emit smoke when open. Billy washed dishes as Lily handed them to him. Leonab dried the dishes, and Stew put them all in various other wall-mounted boxes, opening and closing several doors, though sometimes repeatedly and quite inefficiently.

Once completed, they went upstairs to the large meeting room between the bedrooms. "Who's up for cards?" Billy asked.

"We have five people," responded Diana. "How are we going to play cards with an odd number of people?"

"I'm sure Leonab doesn't know how to play any card games, anyway," Lily said only somewhat derisively.

"That is correct," agreed Leonab sincerely. "I am content to observe your play."

Stew motioned for Leonab to take the seat next to his so he could show her his cards and teach her the basics of the game. Once Billy dealt the first hand, Stew explained that the game was called Spades. "This is an example," he said, holding up the seven of spades.

Casual conversation ebbed and flowed as they shuffled the cards and played again and again. Leonab might have been relieved to have a reprieve of lessons between hands except the casual conversation largely revolved around her background.

As they played, Stew's explanation droned on, much to the chagrin of his opponents, Diana and Lily, but that could have been because they were losing sorely. "You see, Diana led that card in an attempt to set my partner's nil. So, now I should play this card because on the last trick, Billy played the three, and Lily didn't have any of that suit. But Diana didn't realize that I am also out of that suit, which is why I can play this card." Diana always seemed to glance at Stew when he mentioned her name, perhaps a little too eager to respond to some implied request that lingered but remained unspoken. It seemed to Leonab that Diana was hoping for more than Stew's kindness.

"So, Stew will be 37 in a couple of weeks. I'm 30, Diana is 32, and Billy here is 27," Lily said. "How old are you, Leonab?"

"I am unsure exactly wh—" Leonab began.

"Oh, your tribe must not keep birth records," Billy interjected. "Well, you look to be about 25, but with that skin masking your true age, you are probably a little bit older. I'd guess that you're 30 to 35."

"It doesn't matter," Diana said. "You are here with us now. I don't think the Gofsons will kick you out, will they, Stew?" She looked at him with longing eyes.

"Um, no." He swallowed. "No, they won't kick you out regardless of your age or circumstances."

"Hey," Billy said, abandoning the shuffle of the game. "I just thought of what Leonab's explanation of her TV reminded me of." He retrieved his cell phone and began flipping through screens. "Here it is. Listen to this; it's one of my favorites."

Two voices sang in harmony, lamenting a loss. "Now listen to this part," Billy said.

> Some say loneliness and solitude
> Are all that we look forward to
> But speaking from my emptiness
> I can't believe that dreariness
> The poets tell of joys and tears
> Of sorrows, pain, surprise, and fears
> But who can say that this is real?
> And who can tell me what to feel?

"So," said Leonab, "you also have this practice and belief. Are these other prophets of yours?"

"Um, prophet?" questioned Stew, looking to Lily and then Diana.

"Well . . . ," Diana began to explain.

"Billy, is that a Tom and Jerry song?" Lily interrupted.

"No, it's a Joe and Jary song. It's kind of a knockoff. Jary is spelled like Gary with a J. The story is that this guy Joe wrote this song for his son, Jairus, to sing with him in hopes that Tom and Jerry would pick it up and run a second Old Buddies tour. But that didn't work out. It's a classic case of a fan thinking he knows the artist. It's still a great song, though."

"Okay, Leonab, we can talk about prophets tomorrow on our way to the hospital. I'm headed to bed since I guess we've just about called it quits on the game," Stew responded.

"You think?" Lily challenged hotly. "It's only 492 to 87. We can't give you bags or even go blind nil and 10-for-2 to win."

"Good night," Stew responded.

CHAPTER 6

"**D**iana, you are pathetic," Lily criticized. "We might have a chance to beat them someday if you could just get your head out of the clouds. Stew is not interested in you. He'd sooner fall for the not-so-foreign girl here—Leonab." Diana reddened and looked away, nearly bursting into tears.

"Do girls of your t—" Leonab caught herself again. "—culture often address each other so rudely?"

"Yeah. What of it?" Lily responded with hostility.

Leonab pondered this comment. *No wonder the world is doomed.* "Well, I am afraid you are mistaken. I am not available for engagement," she finally said.

"Oh, you're already engaged, huh? Where's the rock?" Lily challenged.

"The what?" Leonab said, puzzled.

"Exactly what I thought. The engagement ring—I didn't see you wearing one. If this guy you're engaged to even exists, he must be some kind of loser."

"Why would I wear a ring to show that I am engaged? Are women of your t—" She caught herself yet again. "—culture accustomed to being treated like property branded by the placement of boundary stones? How many of these stones must each of you bear?"

"No, no," interjected Diana, now drying her eyes and finding herself amused at the ironic interpretation in Leonab's comments. "In our culture, both the man and the woman exchange rings as a symbol of unity with each other. The engagement ring is a promise offered by the man to the woman as a token of his good faith. She wears it as a token of her good faith, the faith of which both have in their mutual promise to each other."

"So if she were to take this ring off, is the promise broken?" Leonab conjectured.

"No, silly. It's just symbolic, like a mutual covenant that they belong to each other."

"I did not see rings on Mr. or Mrs. Gofson," Leonab said, pointing to her nose.

"We wear these rings on our hands, generally on the finger next to the pinkie of the left hand," Diana corrected her.

"Yeah," Lily added, "I had a nose ring, but Mrs. Gofson 'requested' that I take it out while in her house."

"Oh," responded an interested Leonab, "so what does the nose ring represent? Are you someone's property, then, or are you pledged to a cause with this brand?"

"No! It's just a demonstration of self-expression," Lily responded, insulted.

"Oh, so you chose to bear this brand. So what exactly are you expressing with this nose ring?"

"I don't know. That I'm comfortable with who I am, I guess, that I don't have to fit the constraints of society and all," she explained, now with indignity.

"If you were comfortable with who you are, then you wouldn't add or subtract from your appearance, would you? The fact that you have chosen to alter your appearance seems to imply that you are displeased with your family or your looks," Leonab observed.

She didn't realize she had voiced the observation until Lily replied angrily, "Why don't you mind your own business?"

"Oh, I have forgotten my place. Forgive me for speaking so plainly," answered Leonab in a sincere apology.

"Humph!" was Lily's only response. After a brief, uncomfortable silence consisting of Lily glaring at Leonab, Lily went to the restroom, leaving the door ajar so she could listen.

Diana continued to probe. "Are you still interested in hearing about our hot-button issues?"

"Your what?" asked Leonab.

"You know, our topics of contention," Diana replied.

"Oh, yes," responded Leonab with renewed interest.

"It looks like we may be stuck here with her for a while," Lily said, exiting the bathroom, "so why don't we start with an easy one tonight?

"So, we have a bunch of wackos running around our country shooting little kids like a carnival game with assault rifles, and we can't seem to convince the gun lovers to prohibit or even limit gun ownership in order to protect innocent children," Lily began, and then continued in a mock voice. "And the only way to stop a bad guy with a gun is to have a good guy with a gun. How absurd!"

"What exactly is a gun?" Leonab asked.

"Oh, good Lord!" responded an exasperated Lily.

CHAPTER 7

After Lily and Diana gave a long, educational (if condescending) discourse on gun history, laws, and rights, as well as the calamities they have caused in recent history, Diana found a new toothbrush in one of the drawers and showed Leonab how to use it and how to flush the toilet. Leonab figured out showering on her own the next morning and then met Stew in the dining room downstairs.

"Do you want some coffee?" he asked.

She watched as he drank from a cup and decided that was probably what he was offering. "Yes, please."

Diana walked out of the kitchen with a plate of food and sat down at the table. "Sorry, Leonab," said Stew, "you don't have time for breakfast. You'll have to drink the coffee on the way. If you want cream or sugar, it's on the table. Let's get going."

Not having understood exactly what he was saying about cream or sugar, Leonab followed Stew out to his car. He started it up with the push of a button. *Perhaps*, she thought, *this is the hot button Diana mentioned last night. Think about that later,* she admonished herself.

"Who are you going to see at the hospital?" Stew inquired as the car started moving.

"I don't know." She hesitated. "Police Chief Richard Crondell suggested I go there when I told him that I needed to convey a message to your people. He didn't tell me whom I need to see."

"Oh, is that how this came about?" Stew mused.

"Well, he told me that the map location of the white plus sign in the red circle was the hospital and that there were people there who could help me. Then I was on my way, following the paths marked on the map, when I was very nearly trampled by one of these mechanical beasts, fell to the ground, and you found me," Leonab recalled.

"Hmm," Stew said. "I tell you what. Why don't you hang out with me. Just stay out of the way while I work, and maybe you and I can determine who you need to talk to. I have a feeling you won't find what you are looking for here, but we'll know better after we have a chance to talk more."

"Okay," Leonab consented.

"I'm an ER nurse," Stew said. "When people come to the emergency room, they are usually in bad shape, and they experience varying degrees of shock." Leonab listened to Stew's careful explanation of some of his job responsibilities. She had only a basic understanding of all this, but his descriptions were filled with detail upon detail. Stew began describing a recent accident in which apparently two of these cars had collided with one another. One of the drivers perished on site, and Stew had spent a long time attempting to preserve the other's life before he, too, perished. The two drivers were only 22 and 21, which Leonab surmised meant they had not as much experience in life as her most recent acquaintances.

Stew left Leonab in the waiting room of the ER with every intention of checking on her at least every couple of hours. "Just observe for right now. I'll come by in a little while, and maybe we can decide who you need to talk to later."

Leonab was a patient person—she had cultivated this skill—so waiting was nothing new to her. She wasn't aware that Stew had an 18-hour shift ahead of him, and he couldn't have known his day would be complicated with the most accidents Milsap had seen since his volunteer days 16 years ago.

Their district had adjusted to the 18-on, 24-off schedule after a government study was performed showing the 24-hour work shifts were too rigorous on the nervous system and could cause doctors and nurses to suffer delayed reaction times or slowed mental responses to critical situations. The natural adrenaline in one's body could carry one only so far. Weeks were divided into four shifts consisting of three-nurse units plus a doctor. This schedule meant a 72-hour work week, but Stew received an unheard of six weeks of paid vacation per year. His vacation had to be scheduled six months in advance in two-week blocks to ensure that the roaming on-call crews servicing other hospitals could be scheduled, so it was also unheard of for anyone to actually take the six weeks of vacation. Unfortunately, there was a use-it-or-lose-it policy, so Stew's seemingly wonderful perk was really just lipstick on a pig. But at least he really liked this pig. He sincerely did, and he loved helping people in need.

Stew had recently switched to the C shift, which meant that on Friday (today), he started work at 0800 hours and ended Saturday at 0200 hours, and then he worked again Sunday from 0200 hours to 2000 hours. He was hoping to switch back to the A shift or even the D shift to have more of his Sundays free, but he needed to talk with Lou Brockford about it, and he just hadn't gotten around to it.

Stew had grown accustomed to the erratic hours of the shift and made as much of a normal routine of it as he could. He generally tried to sleep around his schedule but as close to normal evening hours as best he could. Fridays were his most regular day because he could sleep a normal night, and then Saturday morning he could sleep from the time he got off until 0800 or 0900 hours. Sundays and Mondays were his worst days because his shift started in the middle of the night and ended when regular people's days began. He had to discipline himself to sleep on Saturday nights and Monday during the day. When he switched shifts, he would just trade one set of good and bad days for another.

Since his shift wouldn't end until 0200 hours, he had anticipated dropping Leonab off with whomever she had intended to meet and then seeing if one of his colleagues getting off the B shift six hours later would take her home, or perhaps imposing on another opportune friend. That idea went out the window when he realized the Police Chief thought Leonab was either an amnesiac or a mental case. *I'll talk with her first to determine how to best proceed*, he thought. *There's no reason for her to be labeled based on a misunderstanding.* He imposed on Sally at the reception desk to keep an eye on Leonab until he could get back to check on her.

Stew had left her in a large room filled with chairs in groups along walls and along some invisible central line, but the chairs in the center faced out toward the other chairs as if those on the outside were to focus on the inside who were, in turn, to observe those on the outside. She sat on the outside, which seemed to make the most sense since she clearly was not one of them. However, she could not distinguish the two groups other than herself. *This is truly an interesting place*, she thought.

There were teevees mounted on side walls near the ceiling so they were visible from every sitting position. On the screens, there were two people sitting behind a table. They were apparently talking, but instead of sound, their message seemed to be printed in blocks at the bottom of the screen. Then the screen changed to another scene with yellow ribbon and what looked like an upturned car resting somewhat precariously in a partially demolished house. She looked around the room as the five people sitting in two groups gasped at the image.

Next to the door with no handles where Stew had exited was a large, square opening in the wall with a lady sitting in front of another teevee with which she seemed to interact. Leonab couldn't tell whether the woman or the teevee initiated the contact, but she was aware of the woman's occasional monitoring.

While she looked around the office, Leonab thought back over her conversation with Diana and Lily from the night before. Lily, it seemed, was very well educated, if opinionated. While Diana was perhaps less educated, she insisted on presenting a balanced view of the issues, practically forcing Lily to present the arguments for both sides. "People use guns to harm other people, individually or en masse, but they also use them for hunting or recreation." How this latter was plausible was beyond Leonab's understanding. Apparently, these guns were also extremely useful in warfare. More than 200 years ago, the present-day United States, which apparently is some sort of three-pronged ruling body that encompasses Milsap, was engaged in a war with the king of the United States and England. After the war was over, the bill came due, and apparently there were 10 itemized rights listed. It must have been very expensive because, as Lily read from some other reference on her cell phone, "freedom is not free." While that seemed like a contradiction, Leonab actually understood the concept as equating to sacrifice.

All this information was somewhat confusing, and she was sure she hadn't gotten the order right or understood the finer details. But when she asked what the 10 items were, Lily insisted on relegating the conversation to the issue at hand.

"The second itemized freedom was the right to bear arms and carry guns," Lily added. "So everyone is entitled to carry guns with a few exceptions, and that basically means everybody is a potential mass murderer." Thinking about the issue that way, Leonab understood why Lily was so opposed to gun ownership. *Since we as people are innately selfish and evil, we are all murderers and criminals in our hearts. Why, then, would we encourage people to own and carry a means for effecting the very evil of their own natures?* Lily and Diana showed Leonab pictures of various guns—big, small, long, and short.

It seemed like this culture's judgment was clouded by their own history. If they were afraid a new king would take over their seemingly complex system of government, then why not continue to select people who value the same things they do? When she heard that this rulership was a profession, she gasped.

"You mean your ancestors fought a war to rid themselves of a king, and now you intentionally select the very same people to rule over you when they are not even common with you?" Leonab exclaimed, exasperated. "Is this not most obtuse? You fought a war to get freedom from a king so you could select those for yourselves who would become elitists and unable to represent you? At least a king in theory represents a true statesman from nobility, meaning his heritage is pride in the land and its people. The rulers you repeatedly select can't possibly be unbiased because it would present a conflict of interest to care for you and provide for themselves. Consider the extravagant cost of these 10 items. Have you not abandoned the very freedoms your ancestors sacrificed to grant you?" *No wonder these people are in trouble,* she thought.

While she recognized the complications their foolish choice of government allowed, it seemed like a good idea in principle. Because of the contradictions and possibility of majority-imposed tyranny, she understood why some might choose to defend their own rights to keep guns, but ultimately, to protect innocent children, she decided to agree with Lily. Guns were bad.

Just then, a man in a dark blue outfit walked in, followed by a woman in a similar outfit. Their apparel was not unlike that of the Police Chief and his subordinates. Leonab watched the pair as they strolled around the room. Finally, curiosity overcame her, and just as they were waiting at the handleless door, she approached them. "Hello. Are you police officers?"

"No, ma'am, not exactly," replied the woman. "We are security officers for the ER. Our shift is about to begin, and we need to get back to relieve the late shift. Do you need help?"

"No, I'm just wondering about the gun you are carrying. I thought if you carried a gun, you also had to bare your arms?" Leonab asked, confused.

Genuine laughter peeled out of the man. "She got you good there, Gates." The door opened, and they walked through as the man continued, "Better bare those arms, Gates. That was a good one."

Leonab remained confused. She must have misunderstood something.

CHAPTER 8

E ven on a slow day, Stew knew he wouldn't have a lot of time to visit with Leonab. Maybe he would have 15 to 20 minutes for a break here or there, and he was hoping at least to poke his head out every once in a while. This was not a slow day or even a normal day; this was a hectic day. All the ERs in their county hospitals had a term for this type of day: Weigh Day. On a Weigh Day, there were so many ambulance runs and patient needs that the doctors and nurses had to weigh the odds of patient survival to prioritize treatment. It felt like a betrayal of the Hippocratic Oath, but he knew the intent was to do the most good to help the sick and abstain from doing harm.

It started with that car that crashed into the house. While Leonab was watching it on the TV in the lobby, the ambulances were arriving at the ER. The driver and two passengers were severely injured, and an elderly woman who was in the house was in critical condition. Stew, having worked at this hospital for as long as he had, still wasn't completely desensitized to the pain and suffering of others. He figured most of his colleagues weren't either; they had just learned to compartmentalize their empathetic reflexes and experience the circumstances of their patients as one might piece together a puzzle. *What is the word for a professional puzzle solver? Mental note to self,* thought Stew, *look that up.* The ER staff were not allowed to use smartphones while on shift except for breaks or at the mandatory 20-minute lunch period. Otherwise, he would just ask Siri.

As he worked through various procedures prepping one of the passengers for immediate surgery, he forced himself to think of how complicated the insurance paperwork would be for this accident. *Would the homeowner's policy cover a flying car if the driver were uninsured?* It was a common practice among ER staff to craft complex scenarios to distract their attention. The crisis was still critical, but the pain and suffering changed to pieces of this challenging puzzle. This one was a particularly unique situation, indeed. *I wonder if the elderly woman lived in the house or was perhaps visiting her grandkids,* he thought. Her injuries were so severe that if their schedule hadn't overlapped with the B shift, she'd probably have been weighed and found wanting. *Look up that passage about the writing on the wall in Daniel later,* thought Stew.

What if this accident had happened a few hours earlier or a few hours after the B shift and before the D shift? What if she'd gotten out of bed earlier or chosen another day to visit? What if? he thought. *Are our lives defined by the "what-if" moments? We can't change the past, I suppose. Ack! What am I thinking about? Avoid empathy.*

As the morning hours slipped away, Stew thought about Leonab and wondered where she had come from. *What is she really doing here?*

Leonab watched as a new group of people entered, immediately followed by the opening of the door with no handles as a lady in a white outfit escorted a boy and a man out to the now-standing group of three. The boy had some sort of firm, white material wrapped around his leg and was using two wooden supports under his arms to assist him in walking. The lady in white spoke with the five-member group for a few moments and then returned to the door. She waved a small card like the spades from the game last night over a red dot to open the door, and she re-exited. Leonab still had not ascertained what was on the other side of that door. She should have looked when those security guards went through, but she was momentarily stunned when they laughed, and her opportunity was lost.

As that group left, Leonab looked on as the lady behind the square opening handed some handheld version of the teevee or large cell phone to the newcomers. It seemed a strange thing to do since one of them was in what appeared to be immense abdominal pain. *What could that teevee possibly do for her abdominal pain?* she wondered. She watched on as the two hobbled over to seats and directed their attention to the device. That seemed like one more inefficiency in her growing list, but this one was extremely unorthodox. She wandered over casually to take a closer look and was appalled to discover that they were printing words on the screen with some unusual writing utensil.

Apparently, in Milsap's culture, before you could help someone, you had to know their name, address, and insurer—whatever that was. *No wonder Yala sent me here; these people are desperate for the message.* Leonab didn't require any of that trivial information to help. Placing her hands on the lady's shoulders, she spoke softly in her own words, gazing intently at the back of the lady's head. The woman began to relax as whatever pain she had began to fade.

"The pain will subside for a while, but you will be fine until you can get long-term help," Leonab said.

The lady was incredulous. "Thank you, deary," she gasped. "I don't know what you said, but that was amazing."

As Leonab walked away, she thought about the manner of the lady's expressed gratitude. *Is it customary to construct sentences with no subject?* She thought through her conversations with the language lessons she'd received in preparation for this assignment. She couldn't remember a single time prior to her encounters in Milsap when such a sentence had been expressed. Last night, Mr. Gofson had held a séance of some sort prior to the meal while holding hands; this was directed to the one they called God and later associated with Yala. *Why did they close their eyes?* she wondered. Well, everyone but Lily had closed their eyes. But when Mr. Gofson expressed gratitude to God, he said "Heavenly father, we thank thee." It was a very refined speech with formal language. She wondered if this God did not speak the common vernacular. *We thank thee and thank you,* she thought. *Who is doing the thanking in the latter? How does this passive expression of gratitude convey personal appreciation? It doesn't.*

If God is really the same as Yala, though, she thought, *then he speaks all languages.* Maybe she could spend some time investigating this God. Maybe she could find one of these cell phones or borrow one, but someone would also have to teach her how to use it. *It can't be that difficult, can it?*

CHAPTER 9

By the time Stew came out to see Leonab, he was apologizing profusely for having abandoned her for the past six hours. He handed her some wrapped nuts and a cold metal cylinder that he snapped open. "Are you doing okay? I don't have long to chat because we are really slammed today. Do you want me to have someone take you back to the house? I won't be off for another 12 hours."

Leonab accepted the proffered package and cylinder, and immediately asked, "Can I borrow your cell phone to research your God?"

"Huh? Oh, um, sorry, I left my cell back in my locker," Stew apologized. "What have you been doing out here anyway? Are you sure you don't want to go back to the house?"

"Well, this is a very exciting place. I am most interested, however, in learning more about your particular God and associated beliefs," replied Leonab.

"Okay. Well, there's a New Testament on that side table. It will tell you all about my beliefs." Stew walked over to pick up the

Bible and then brought it back to Leonab. "Here, start in the book of John. Maybe later we can talk about it. If you need anything, let Sally at the desk know, okay?"

"I will do so," she promised.

As Stew returned to the back, an eighth ambulance pulled in with one more crisis. The several patients who had come through the front lobby didn't seem to be in critical pain at all, but though their symptoms were not serious, their issues were as serious as any normal ER visit. They all claimed that the foreign girl in the lobby had prayed over them prior to being ushered back. He could kick himself for not having questioned her more specifically about what she'd been doing out there. Maybe he could get a quick message to Sally at the desk to see if she knew what was going on.

"In the beginning was the Word, and the Word was with God, and the Word was God."

As Leonab read, she found herself puzzling over the words. She saw the name Jesus Christ, who was apparently the one to whom Mrs. Gofson had referred in defining Christianity. *What does he have to do with the Word at the beginning? Why are some of the letters in red? If there is a connection between Yala and God or Jesus Christ, some of the names mentioned in this book may be English names of prophets I've read in my own language.* She got confused when reading the comments about being "born again" and skipped on to the next numbered section.

As she continued, she found herself identifying with Jesus when he said, "My food . . . is to do the will of him who sent me and to finish his work."

Isn't that my job, too? she thought. *Had not Yala sent me with a message just as he had sent Ezza?* "Go and proclaim my message to my people. You are not being sent to a distant land with people of strange speech." *Or Yesheme?* "I have called you before your beginning to be a prophet to your people." She, of course, had been called to a foreign people in a different time.

Maybe this Jesus was a prophet like Jwo, of whom she had never heard. *But why, then, does he seem to talk to God as his actual father? He has as much power in working miracles as any of the prophets. Is this a lost book? Is my mission really to discover this book of prophecy for my own people?* She noted that Jesus spoke so often with confidence proclaiming, "I am."

She looked up as the door opened again and watched as the same scene repeated itself, with Sally handing over the portable teevee to some poor, suffering individual and his companion. *Can God be the same as Yala if Stew and Mr. and Mrs. Gofson, who seemingly profess to follow him, are not willing or not able to help the hurting and aid those who are in need?*

Sally watched as Stew's dark-colored friend approached the new patients who were busy filling out their required paperwork. The patients were visibly uncomfortable as she approached, and when she reached out, they nearly buried their chairs into the wall to avoid her touch. "Help," the injured man called, "I am being assaulted!"

"Please," Leonab said, "I am here to help you."

"Nurse!" the new patient screamed. "Get this woman away from me!"

Sally didn't know what to do. Legally, she should call the security guards, but she felt a professional courtesy to tell Stew first. Unfortunately, this Leonab was exacerbating the situation and would not leave well enough alone. Sally radioed a message to Stew and called the security guards.

"I'm sorry, ma'am," said the security guard called Gates. "You're going to have to leave."

"I have helped a lot of people here today. For which of these are you evicting me? I am here to help these people," Leonab responded.

"Look, lady," the other security officer reprimanded. "We're asking you to leave for making yourself out to be some kind of psycho doctor. You're not wanted here, and you can't practice your quack healing techniques in the hospital."

As Leonab was trying to figure out what to do and how to contact Stew, he came hurrying out. "Hey, Sally told me you were getting kicked out of the lobby. What were you doing?" He didn't pause for a response. "Look, it's only 1730 hours; I don't get off for another eight and a half hours. I'll see if one of the ambulance crews can take you home. Wait here a couple minutes."

A few moments later, an older guy came around the building and introduced himself as Jack Stubbard. "Stew asked me to take you back to his house. Come. Get in the ambulance, and I'll run you that way. With a day like the one we've had today, we'll be lucky to get you there before I get another call." As she followed him to the much bulkier, red box of a car, she first noticed his outfit and then those of the other two people in the box car.

Jack was disappointed that Leonab didn't ask him to use the siren all the way to the Gofsons' house. She just seemed to take in

46

the chatter between them and the noise from the radio. He decided to make an attempt at conversation. "Do you know the toughest part about this job?" When she didn't respond, he continued, "It's not the tragedy of accidents or even that of intentional maladies inflicted by one person on another. And it's not the emotional toll exacted by the responsibility of constantly making life-and-death decisions. Those things certainly weigh heavily on my heart. But the worst part about this job is knowing that no matter how much we want to or how hard we try, we can't save them all."

She continued in silence, so he gave up until they pulled up to the house a few minutes later. "Hope to see you around," he said.

"I thank you, sir," she said, and walked to the door of the house, thinking of another sentence with no subject as well as the gravity of the day's events.

CHAPTER 10

Leonab was distracted when she wandered in, but she noticed that the table was set and that Lily, Diana, and Billy were stumbling down the stairs. She wondered what they had been doing all day. Maybe she could investigate that later, but she realized that her total consumption for the day had consisted of a cup of bitter black liquid, a metal cup of sweet juice, and a bag of dried nuts. As the others sat at the table, she joined them.

Mrs. Gofson noticed her and brought out additional tableware without acknowledging her presence. Mr. Gofson exited from the side room carrying a large, heavy pot while wearing some padded gloves. Mrs. Gofson set a wooden tray or crate on the table, and he set the pot on it. She then produced a basket of bread. Then Mr. and Mrs. Gofson sat. With Stew absent, she had to reach farther to hold hands with Mrs. Gofson. Even though his chair was removed from the table, his absence was felt as much as seen.

After Mr. Gofson led the ritual séance over the table, Mrs. Gofson passed the bread to Leonab and motioned her to pass it to Diana. Mr. Gofson began serving soup in the bowls one by one. Once everyone was served, they began eating. Though Leonab was curious to know what interesting events were going on here, her patient nature prevented her from asking a thousand questions. She also wanted to study more about God and thought that perhaps Mr. and Mrs. Gofson would answer some of her questions. Then there were also the topics the girls were going to help her understand. *There is just so much to take in, but how do I find the right opportunity to share the message with these people?*

With all these thoughts cluttering her mind, Leonab hadn't heard the conversation around her, which apparently had paused in anticipation of her input. "I am sorry," she politely said.

"Oh, we were just asking how your meeting at the hospital went," said Mrs. Gofson.

"Well, when we arrived, Stew wanted to help determine who I needed to see first," Leonab replied. "However, he was very busy, so I didn't get to meet with anyone today."

"How did you get back?" asked Diana.

"Stew asked Jack Stubbard to bring me home in the large, red box car," she readily replied.

"You rode home in the ambulance?" Billy asked. "That's cool. Did he turn on the lights and siren to bring you home?"

"Escorting a lady home is hardly an emergency, Billy," Mrs. Gofson chided. "Perhaps Mr. Gofson and I can discuss your situation with you after dinner, dear."

"That would be most helpful," Leonab responded, and then hazarded a question. "While I was at the hospital, I read some of the Bible that Stew loaned me. He suggested starting somewhere in the front part but not quite the beginning; John was the name. It told about a man named Jesus Christ, to whom I assume you were referring last night. I didn't finish, but at one point, Jesus asked this question to a man who couldn't walk: 'Do you want to get well?' Why did he ask that question? Are there people in your culture who do not want to get well?"

"What a splendid question, and so informed," a delighted Mr. Gofson said. "Interestingly enough, this is one of the primary issues in the upcoming election for mayor of Milsap."

Lily's posture and demeanor became visibly hostile at this, and Diana became uncomfortable.

"You see," continued Mr. Gofson, "as you have rightly postulated, not everyone actually wants help. People can be divided into two classes: number one, those who need help themselves, and number two, those who have the means to help others. Each of these classes can be further subdivided into two categories: One-A represents those people who need help and know and want it, and they therefore pursue it to become members of class two. One-B represents those people who need help but either don't know it or don't want it, and they therefore seek only to take from those around them. Two-A represents those people who have the means to help others and are willing to help those of class one. Two-B represents those people who have the means to help others but are unwilling to do so. Members of categories one-A and two-A are generally those who accept responsibility for their own actions and wish to help others do the same. Members of categories one-B and two-B are selfish, wanting others to provide for them or wanting someone else to take care of the needs of others, such as the government."

That all seemed overly complex to Leonab.

"There are certainly variations within these classes and categories. I'm oversimplifying the matter, but basically, we all wind up somewhere on this scale," Mr. Gofson went on. "Mrs. Gofson and I are in group two-A because God has blessed us with enough to take care of our own needs, and we feel compelled, then, to help others. Those who come into our home, such as you all"—Mr. Gofson motioned around the table—"represent class one-A because you recognize that you need help and are willing to seek it out so you can become members of class two-A."

Leonab looked at Lily, Diana, and Billy and said quizzically, "I didn't realize you were all sick."

Lily was just about to explode. "Being poor is not the same as being sick!"

"Yes, I meant in the metaphorical sense," Mr. Gofson interrupted. "You see, Leonab, Jesus came to help people help themselves. That's why he told the lame man to get up and walk after he claimed he wanted to be healed."

"So, in the upcoming election, we have two candidates for mayor," interjected an impatient Mrs. Gofson, trying to get the conversation back on track and bring closure to Mr. Gofson's original line of reasoning. "One candidate believes that the poor should work their way up from poverty with the support of benevolent individuals in the community, and the other believes the government should give out free money, food, healthcare, and various other services irregardless of the person's initiatives."

Leonab was momentarily distracted by the inefficiency of the word *irregardless*. *Isn't the extra syllable at the beginning superfluous?* she thought.

"We believe that Mr. Ludlow would enslave the poor people of our society by giving them their basic needs for free without having them earn them. In the same way, he would enslave the working people of our society to pay for those needs. He believes the government is the best manager of an individual's resources. He wants to think for the people; he's making himself a god. Our beliefs align more closely with those of Mrs. Albright who wants the government to stay out of the human welfare business and allow institutions such as churches and charities to take care of people," Mr. Gofson said.

"Which we practice," added Mrs. Gofson.

Lily was frustrated and replied, "Why should a needy person have to seek out the basic needs for survival? Are we no better than cavemen who struggled to make fire for warmth? Haven't we as a society progressed in our understanding of human decency and communal responsibility? Are these rights not granted to us by our creator? Why, then, do we have to beg and plead for them, depending on the charity of strangers? If the government recognizes that we have these rights, then the government is also responsible for ensuring that we receive these rights. Otherwise, the statement is hollow. We can't depend on good-natured, well-meaning, religious individuals and institutions to not abuse or manipulate those who are at their mercy."

Leonab noted mentally that both Mr. Gofson and Lily were concerned about abuses. Mr. Gofson was concerned that the government would manipulate the citizens, while Lily was concerned that charities would manipulate those in need. No matter how passionately they argued, it seemed like they both agreed on one fundamental principle: those in authority are in a position to take advantage of their subjects.

"Through the government, we can choose our leadership, who will ensure that our rights are not abused," Lily concluded.

Mrs. Gofson, who had patiently listened to Lily's diatribe, responded kindly. "You are encouraged and welcome to hold and voice your own opinions in this house, Lily, but you will do so civilly."

"Those in need do have their choice of charities," responded Mr. Gofson. "If they are concerned that one group is abusing them, they can go to another institution. But the fundamental principle is that people have to work for what they get; otherwise, they won't appreciate it. God helps those who help themselves."

Diana interrupted, "I don't think that's in the Bible."

"Well, not in that precise verbiage," said Mr. Gofson, "but the principles are there. Paul said, 'The one who is unwilling to work shall not eat.' You see, God expects you to put feet to your prayers."

"But remember when Abraham tried to 'put feet to his prayers' to have a kid? That didn't work out right, did it?" Diana challenged. "Paul also presents a sort of contradiction when he says that 'every man shall bear his own burden.' He also said to carry each other's burdens. I think we have to find a middle ground somewhere."

"Yes, well, those were specific circumstances, like women not speaking in church—it applied to their specific culture," Mr. Gofson replied. "And as for Abraham, he chose the wrong direction to walk in. Obviously, he had to continue engaging with his wife in order for God to give him a child. It's not like that was going to happen on its own, right? Well, except for Jesus and Mary."

Leonab hadn't heard any of the conversation after Mr. Gofson said that God expected her to put feet to her prayers. *While I am seated*, she thought, *I can easily put my feet down, up, or elsewhere, but I am sitting at rest. If I were active, however, it would be impossible to put my feet anywhere other than where they are required to be.* Being at rest didn't seem consistent with Mr. Gofson's premise that one should be actively working for one's own interest. *Perhaps I am just overanalyzing this confusing and inefficient language.*

Leonab noticed that everyone seemed engaged in the discussion except Billy, who was silently stirring the remnants of his soup. She wondered what he thought about all this. Then she remembered what Jack had said when he dropped her off: You can't save them all. What did he mean by that phrase? *Maybe that's why Jesus asked his question to the lame man, because he knew what Jack Stubbard knew.*

With supper ending, Mrs. Gofson said, "Lily, Diana, and Billy, please clear the dishes, and take care of the kitchen. Leonab, why don't we retire to the living room to discuss your situation?"

CHAPTER 11

Leonab followed Mr. and Mrs. Gofson into the room with the large teevee and was ushered into a seat across from a low-standing table. As soon as she sat, she noted again that the blank teevee screen had the most prominent position in the room because the Gofsons and she would have to turn slightly away from it and toward each other to engage in face-to-face conversation. She stared for a moment at the blank screen and pondered her own emptiness, her inability to help that final group of people in the hospital. *It wasn't for lack of desire on my part or lack of ability on the part of Yala; it was the unwillingness on the part of those in need. Perhaps Mr. Gofson was partially right about the classes or categories of people.* "You can't help them all," she whispered.

Mrs. Gofson began. "Now, we don't know what kind of trouble you are in, but we may be able to help. Let's start with where you are really from. Are you from Mexico or Honduras? If you are an illegal immigrant, let us know now because there are certain procedures we will have to follow. While we want to provide you with everything you need, we also can't be involved in legal disputes."

"Oh, for heaven's sake, Edna," said Mr. Gofson. "Her English is better than Billy's. She's clearly not an illegal immigrant."

"What is an immigrant?" Leonab asked.

"Immigration," responded Mr. Gofson, "is another critical issue in the upcoming mayoral election. It involves the ingress into our country of people who are not US citizens. This is a complex issue for us. While we want to help all people, the Bible also instructs us to obey the authority God has established over us. Many people in our congregation believe illegal immigrants come to this country and specifically to our city to receive the benefits and freedoms of our society without having contributed to it."

"You mean that the bill for the 10 rights is not for all people?" Leonab asked, confused.

"That is what some people believe," answered Mrs. Gofson. "Basically, they believe God blessed Americans to be here and receive American benefits just as he blesses other people in their own countries according to their own actions."

"And this is what God teaches you?" Leonab asked.

"Well, that's complicated," answered Mr. Gofson. "The Bible is somewhat conflicted on that. You see, the Old Testament suggests that we should care for the foreigner, but the New Testament tells us that God has placed our rulers over us, and we are to respect them. So, obeying God's Old Testament commands may cause us to violate his New Testament commands. Since we believe the old things have passed, we lean toward trying to honor the new commands."

"Do you use drugs or alcohol, Leonab?" asked Mrs. Gofson.

"What are drugs and alcohol?" Leonab was bewildered.

"They are mind-altering chemicals that people inject or otherwise consume to affect their mental state," answered Mr. Gofson.

Mrs. Gofson continued. "We understand that many people need medications, and we're not opposed to doctor-prescribed medicines, but illegal drugs and alcohol consumption are strictly prohibited in our home."

"I'm not engaged in any such behavior," responded Leonab.

"Okay. I believe we have established that she is not a serious threat, Edna," Mr. Gofson said, somewhat derisively. "Now, Leonab, perhaps you can tell us what brings you to Milsap."

Just then a bell rang in the house. Mrs. Gofson got up and opened the front door. "Mayor Anderson," she greeted the new visitor. "What a pleasant surprise!" The new gentleman entered the room and shook hands with Mr. Gofson.

"I'm just stopping by to make sure you are picking up the banner for the mayoral debate," said Mayor Anderson.

"Yes, I will be sending Stew and Billy tomorrow afternoon. Why don't you join us for a few minutes? Meet Leonab, our newest guest. Leonab, this is Mayor Anderson. He's one of the most prominent members of our congregation. Leonab is a newcomer to Milsap, staying with us until she gets on her feet. She was just about to tell us what brought her here."

Leonab thought about this. *Perhaps the mayor is the right person to hear the message.* "I have come to bring a message to the people of Milsap," started Leonab, "a message about your future."

Mayor Anderson was up and moving toward the door in a hurry with Mr. Gofson at his heels. Leonab heard the mayor say, "Is she some kind of environmental wacko or something? What kind of operation are you running here, Henry? I don't tell you what to preach on Sundays; you keep your circus of a household from telling me how to run the city."

When Mr. Gofson returned, Leonab asked, "What is an environmental wacko?"

"That's another of the complex issues dividing our city. The out-wing side of the argument is that if we don't take care of the environment, our children and their children will be breathing smog or living underground, while the in-wing side believes this is an extreme projection meant to manipulate and control society. However, while the out-wing group claims to want to protect the children of the future, they are also in support of abortion—the killing of unborn children—which the in-wing group is opposed to," Mr. Gofson explained.

"I'm not talking about the environment, though Y— the Great One does tell us to take care of the world he created. What do you mean by killing unborn children?" Leonab asked, horrified.

"When a woman gets pregnant in circumstances that are undesirable, she can go to a doctor or medical facility to have the baby terminated," Mrs. Gofson answered. "This position is labeled pro-choice because it allows the woman to choose what will happen to her own body."

"What about the life and body of the child and the child's future choices?" Leonab asked.

"Those of us who value the life of the unborn child over the choices of the woman are called pro-life," Mrs. Gofson replied.

"I suppose we could call ourselves pro-choices based on your comment," Mr. Gofson interrupted. "Surely a child with a full life ahead of him or her would have more choices remaining than a woman of childbearing age."

Leonab was disturbed by the thought of people in this society who believed that whether someone lived or died was a decision to be made for convenience. She thought of her own daughter,

Bontaq. "Are you talking about the people who kill innocent children? Are these the same as the gun lovers?"

"Gun rights is a separate issue entirely. Many of our constituents identify as in-wing. A person's right to own a gun is granted by the Bill of Rights. People need to be able to protect themselves from others and ultimately from the possibility that the government would try to impose tyrannical polices again. Just because some people choose to abuse certain rights doesn't mean that everyone's rights should be restricted."

Leonab saw a glimpse of Diana as she was heading upstairs. Leonab felt confused by all of this and wondered, *Are these issues of drugs, immigration, and abortion as important to Lily and Diana?* Then she remembered what she was reading in the Bible. "Will you lend me a Bible so I can read more about Jesus Christ?"

"Sure, let me get you one," replied Mr. Gofson. As he returned, he said, "Now, be careful how you read this. Interpretation can be tricky. Mrs. Gofson, Stew, or I would be happy to help you understand what you are reading. Look here in the front. There's a table of contents so you can pick up where you left off."

CHAPTER 12

Leonab started up the stairs, somewhat overwhelmed with the strange conversation she'd just had with the Gofsons. When she reached the top, she found Billy alone in the large meeting room, shuffling cards. She sat next to him at the table and laid the Bible beside her.

After sitting quietly for a moment, she asked, "I noticed you were particularly quiet at dinner. What do you think about all these political topics?"

Billy shrugged and shifted his gaze from the cards to look at her. "I don't much care. I suppose as long as I'm here, I should do the errands for Mr. and Mrs. Gofson, go to church with them, and respect their beliefs. I can't much complain. Don't bite the hand that feeds you, right?"

"So you are completely apathetic to political issues that seem to be so important to the others around you? In what way is that respectful? To respect someone else's position, you must first consider the issues, ponder the implications, understand the arguments presented, and share your own convictions or conclusions. By not doing so, you are no more respectful than the table that allows anyone to build upon it," Leonab responded directly.

"Yeah, well, to each his or her own; that's my motto," quipped Billy sharply. "Live and let live."

"More like live and let die, heh, Billy?" interjected Lily, who had just opened the bedroom door.

"Lily, how could you?" exclaimed Diana from just behind her.

Leonab watched as tears began to well in Billy's eyes. He set his cards down on the table, slowly stood, and walked toward the other bedroom door.

Somewhat remorseful, Lily followed him. "I was just joking, Billy. I didn't mean it like that." As Billy slammed the door in her face, her voice rose to a shout. "I'm sorry, all right?"

"What were you thinking, Lily?" asked an irate Diana in a hushed but furious tone. "I can't believe you said that! How many times have I told you that you have to be more sensitive—you're as bad as the Gofsons. At least with them, they understand that a person's view on policy must be tempered when dealing with individuals. No matter what your personal views on political issues or how smart you are, you have to consider where your audience is mentally, psychologically, and physically."

"I know, I know, all right? I said I was sorry," Lily responded.

"Look," Diana said, her voice softening, "I know you don't buy into all that Jesus stuff, but you and I have both agreed that he seemed like a good teacher and that some of the things he said make sense." When Lily consented grudgingly, Diana continued, "Remember that story when Lazarus died and his two sisters went to see Jesus because he hadn't shown up in time? They both said the same thing, something like this: 'Jesus, you're too late. If you would have come sooner, my brother wouldn't have died.' Jesus, however, read the social cues you are missing. To Martha, he presented a challenge, and to Mary, he responded with compassion. Whether we believe what he said or even if it made any sense isn't important. Learn the lesson about paying attention to people, and relegate the expression of your political views to your own proverbial pulpit."

"Okay, okay." Lily walked to Billy's door and knocked. "Billy, can we talk?"

"Go away," came Billy's response.

"Look, I'm really sorry. That was completely insensitive of me. I let my stupid intellect supersede my mental filter." No response came from the other side of the door. "I'm here for you when you're ready to talk about it; just call or text me."

Diana and Leonab followed Lily as she headed into the other bedroom. "What was that all about?" Leonab asked. "I couldn't get him to show any emotion or even take anything seriously, and with your seemingly innocuous statement, you drove him to tears."

Diana responded as Lily went into the bathroom to wash her face. "Well, Billy's dad abandoned him when he was a baby. Lily and I met him about eight years ago when he was 19. He and his mom didn't have much and lived hand to mouth."

Hand to mouth—is that related to biting the hand that feeds you? wondered Leonab.

Diana was still explaining when Leonab consciously suppressed that thought. " . . . town to town and from man to man. Through all of this, his mom was desperately depressed and eventually decided she didn't want to go on living. She talked to Billy about it in her incoherent way."

Lily came out of the bathroom and picked up the story where Diana left off. "In this country, we have the right to life, liberty, and the pursuit of happiness. It's part of the Declaration of Independence that we mentioned last night. The educated of our society understand that this right also extends to a choice of when to end one's life—live or let die."

"Wait." Leonab raised her hand. "You mean you have the ability to kill yourself?"

"Choose to end your own life with dignity," Lily corrected.

"Dignity?" retorted Leonab. "Dignity is a characteristic of the living. Dying with dignity means living to the end naturally through a long, hard-fought battle, whether against physical foe or internal struggles. Choosing death is no noble action. How can you justify people ending their own lives, shirking the responsibilities life has entrusted to them? It seems akin to the killing of innocent children—just look at how his mom's decision has affected Billy's life."

Lily stopped for a moment and then responded. "No, Billy is responsible for his own decisions."

Diana looked directly at Lily and said, "Are you saying that Billy is responsible for himself?"

Somewhat uncertain, Lily responded, "Yeah, his mom's choice was hers to make. She can do whatever she wants with her body."

"Okay," Diana said, "so if Billy is responsible for himself, then your position on the government's responsibility to take care of him is now untenable."

"What, wait. People like Billy need the government's help to take care of themselves. You're twisting the meaning of my words."

"It seems to me that the personal choices granted to individuals by your government or the creator are often in conflict with what is good for the community," Leonab said before Lily and Diana could begin to argue. "Would people like Billy require government assistance if this same government had protected or assisted his mother rather than granting her the right to kill herself?"

Lily and Diana thought about this, but before they managed a verbal response, Leonab followed up with another statement. "Your comment about a woman having the right to choose what happens to her body reminds me of something the Gofsons said about abortion . . . "

Lily jumped on the new topic. "Yes, the Gofsons are extremely anti-women's rights. They practically believe that women are enslaved to their bodies rather than the masters of them."

"What Lily is saying," interrupted Diana, "is that we don't really know when life begins, so abortion is a way to end a potential life. As women, we should have ultimate control over our own bodies. That's why we are pro-choice."

"When a woman is pregnant, does she not feel kicks from the baby?" Leonab asked.

"Well, yes, but that's later in the pregnancy," said Diana pensively.

"Does she not sense additional hunger?" questioned Leonab. "Surely that urge for additional sustenance and the weight gain are not a response of her body alone."

"Well, the changes happen to that particular woman's body," said Diana, now somewhat defensively.

"It seems to be another contradiction to say we shouldn't let people have guns because they have the potential to kill innocent children and simultaneously say a woman has the right to kill a potential child much earlier."

Lily looked appalled. Diana shook her head and said, "Remember when you were talking with the Gofsons? I didn't overhear much of the conversation, but since I was the last one out of the kitchen, I heard Mr. Gofson telling you that just because some people abuse their rights doesn't mean you can withhold those same rights from everyone."

Leonab thought about this statement. It sounded reasonable, but she found it odd that two groups who apparently didn't agree on fundamental issues would use very similar logic to justify their own self-contradicting beliefs.

CHAPTER 13

Leonab fell asleep quickly, having been immersed in all the new culture and conflict, but she awoke to the sound of blaring music. When she looked up, she noticed Lily was gone but Diana was still sound asleep.

Getting up to walk to the window, she saw Stew's car pulling in with the transparent portions apparently broken out. Before he turned the car off, she heard these words:

> We shout your name, shout your name
> Filling up the skies with endless praise, endless praise
> Yahweh, Yahweh, we love to shout . . .

Stew stumbled out of the car and closed the door. Then he opened the door again and did something to return the transparent portions of the doors. He closed the door and then started toward the house.

Leonab tiptoed out and noticed that the other bedroom door was also open. *Billy must be up, too.* She quietly slipped downstairs and proceeded to the front door where she expected to find Stew.

After failing to see him, she opened the door herself. There she found Stew standing and talking quietly with Billy and Lily, both seated on the front stairs.

"... discussing a difference of opinion," she heard Billy say.

"Okay," Stew said, "let me know if you solve world hunger, but make sure you leave some of the world's problems for me to resolve. I'm off for the next 24 hours." Stew looked up and saw Leonab standing at the door. "I'll see y'all in a few hours; I'm headed to bed."

As Stew and Leonab stepped inside and closed the door, Stew asked, "Leonab, what are you doing up?"

"I heard your music; it was rather loud," she said. "Then I heard some of the words. I think I understood all of them except 'Yah-way.' What is that?"

"Yahweh," Stew corrected her. "It's one of the names of God, only we don't really know how to pronounce it for sure. Anyway, we can talk about it in a couple hours after I've had time to rest. Oh, and we need to talk about this morning—yesterday morning—in the ER."

"Oh yes, I have a lot of questions about what you suggested I read in the Bible," Leonab agreed.

"Okay, good night," Stew said.

Leonab followed Stew up the stairs, figuring that Lily and Billy were resolving their interpersonal issues and would not want to be interrupted. When she lay down, she couldn't seem to sleep as the name Stew had mentioned kept coming back to her. Yahweh—could he be the same as Yala?

She decided to resign her feeble attempt to sleep and instead pick up where she'd left off reading the Bible. After returning to the large room where she'd left the Bible, she realized this one seemed much bigger than the one she had been reading at the ER. Looking in the front at the table of contents Mr. Gofson had shown her, she found that John was listed four times. She found the first one, and though the words were a little more formal than those she'd read earlier, they were, in fact, the same. She decided to look up the other books named John and found that they were much shorter, so she began reading 1 John.

Here, the author also spoke of the beginning and mentioned the Word once again, although this time, it was the Word of Life. As Leonab continued to read, she realized a change in the tone from the previous reading. It seemed that John was now writing about Jesus Christ rather than telling about events and experiences during his life. She stopped for a moment when she read, "The blood of Jesus Christ his Son cleanseth us from all sin."

What does that mean? she thought. *Apparently, Jesus Christ is the Son of God.* John said that here and in the verses she had read earlier. *How could I not be aware?* She puzzled again and then read on. The words were so simple, yet they were also profound.

The darkness is past, and the true light now shineth.

Whosoever denieth the Son, the same hath not the Father.

Behold, what manner of love the Father hath bestowed upon us, that we should be called the sons of God.

Beloved, let us love one another: for love is of God; and every one that loveth is born of God, and knoweth God. . . . Herein is love, not that we loved God, but that he loved us, and sent his Son to be the propitiation for our sins.

*These things have I written unto you that believe on
the name of the Son of God; that ye may know that ye
have eternal life, and that ye may believe on the name
of the Son of God.*

She continued poring over the words, completing 2 John and
3 John and then reading through the following one-page book of
Jude. When she turned the page, she found herself looking at the
book of Revelation. Since she wanted to focus on what Stew had
recommended to her, she decided to return to the original John.
But before she flipped back, she saw the name John at the end of
the very first sentence.

*The Revelation of Jesus Christ . . . sent . . . unto his
servant John.*

Prophecy! she thought. She decided to continue reading after
all. There was now no doubt that Jesus (*is he the Word?*) was
somehow the same as God, and they were also related to the Holy
Ghost, which must be the same as the Spirit of God. John had said
this earlier:

*For there are three that bear record in heaven, the
Father, the Word, and the Holy Ghost: and these three
are one.*

But she wasn't yet wholly convinced that this God whom
Stew called Yahweh was the one true Yala.

I am Alpha and Omega . . . the first and the last.

There is that phrase "I am" again. That phrase stood out to
Leonab since Jesus had used it a few times. He seemed to convey

such confidence. Reading on, she noted that since this book was prophecy, much of it probably wouldn't make sense to her anyway. *Prophecy is usually encrypted*, she thought, so she wasn't fazed by what seemed to be proclamations of future events. She was certain she was not the specific recipient of these messages, though if Yahweh were Yala, then eventually they would affect her, too.

> *And they sung a new song, saying, Thou art worthy to take the book, and to open the seals thereof: for thou wast slain, and hast redeemed us to God by thy blood out of every kindred, and tongue, and people, and nation.*

At this point, Lily and Billy came up the stairs. They each said good night to her as they parted company.

When Leonab returned to her reading, she saw the names Gog and Magog with a discussion of a final battle. She stopped. She had seen many names and knew she was unfamiliar with the English versions of places and people, but these two names were names in her own language. She could not believe it. She knew that Yala would go to battle against Gog and Magog because she'd read another prophet's words foretelling this event.

As she continued, she was overcome with grief as the living were judged and then the dead. All were standing at the Great White Throne. Then she found hope.

> *And I saw a new heaven and a new earth. . . . And God shall wipe away all tears from their eyes; and there shall be no more death, neither sorrow, nor crying, neither shall there be any more pain: for the former things are passed away. And he that sat upon the throne said, Behold, I make all things new.*

*It is done. I am Alpha and Omega, the beginning
and the end. I will give unto him that is athirst of the
fountain of the water of life freely.*

*Didn't Jesus offer to give someone water from an eternal
fountain in my earlier reading?* she thought.

When she finished reading Revelation, she thought she should
go back to bed, but the sun was up. She was excited about what
she was learning, though it didn't seem to coincide with what she
was experiencing in this time. She now had information about a
future beyond this time and hers. Now she grasped her purpose
here more fully, but since she wanted to read more of John, she
turned back and found where she had left off.

*He that is without sin among you, let him first cast a
stone at her.*

*Woman, where are those thine accusers? Hath no
man condemned thee?*

*She said, No man, Lord. And Jesus said unto her,
Neither do I condemn thee: go, and sin no more.*

*I am the light of the world: he that followeth me shall
not walk in darkness, but shall have the light of life.*

*I am the good shepherd: the good shepherd giveth his
life for the sheep.*

*Oh, here's that story Diana was talking about. Wait, did Jesus
just let his friend Lazarus die? You can't save them all. Surely Yala
could save them all; surely Yala wouldn't let his friend die. Jesus is
practically rude to Martha when he replies to her question "Where*

were you?" with "I am the resurrection and the life." When Mary says the same thing, why does he cry instead?

Oh, wow! He calls the dead to life? Surely he is Yala.

But why would Yala make himself a servant and wash his followers' feet? What does he mean that one of his friends would betray him?

> *I am the way, the truth, and the life: no man cometh unto the Father, but by me.*

Is the Comforter the same as the Holy Ghost or Spirit of God? Why does Jesus talk so much about going away? Where is he going that they can't follow him unless they lay down their own lives? Maybe he's leaving to prepare his army for the battle at Gog and Magog. No, that can't be right because that is definitely in the future, and this has to be part of history.

Why does Judas betray Jesus? Peter obviously has weapons training. Why does Jesus not want him to fight this battle? How could Jesus get arrested?

Diana stepped out of the bedroom, closing the door softly behind her, and greeted Leonab.

CHAPTER 14

"Good morning," said Diana. "Couldn't sleep?"

Another sentence with no subject, thought Leonab. "Well, when Stew returned, he was playing loud music, and I woke up and started reading some more." Leonab held up the Bible she had been reading, using both hands to manage its bulk.

"Oh, anything interesting?" inquired Diana.

"Well, I just read about Lazarus dying and how Jesus treated the sisters differently," Leonab responded. "That didn't make sense to me, but I thought about what you'd said about people being different and requiring different types of engagements. Then Jesus raised Lazarus from the dead. That was awesome!"

"Yeah, I'm not sure how much of that to believe," Diana countered. "On a separate topic, I was thinking about what you said about abortion and gun control—you know, how the first kills the children that the other only might kill. Well, don't you think that's kind of offensive? I mean, lots of women have had abortions over the past few decades for various reasons, and you're basically calling them all murderers."

"Diana, we all make choices every day. Nearly all our choices affect other people. Take that scenario with Billy's mom. She thought her decision was best for her and everyone else, but we know now that it clearly was not. You read me some of Jwo's prophecies, remember? You can't change the past. However, I'm not sure if Jwo finished this thought: 'You can't let the past control your future.' The past is not meant to define you. All of those experiences are meant to refine you into who Y— God wants you to become. Don't forget yesterday's lessons, but don't make yesterday's mistakes. And it is our job to help others not make the same mistakes we have made. God promises forgiveness when we seek him, but there is a coming judgment. When would you prefer me to tell you about the judgment—before or after the fact?"

Diana looked somewhat dejected. "I'm ashamed to tell you that I had an abortion."

"We are all ashamed of things we do, choices we make," said Leonab as she got up and hugged Diana to provide comfort.

"I know we all make mistakes, but you're saying I killed a child." Diana began to cry. "Doesn't that make me evil? Sure, it's in the past, and I don't want to repeat that mistake if I can even get pregnant again. Sure, I want to help others make better choices, but it doesn't change who I am, what I've done. I am a murderer just like those gunmen at the school." Diana was weeping uncontrollably now.

"No, Diana," Leonab countered, "you are not defined by your mistakes. You have matured, changed—you are being refined into who God is making you."

"But how can God ever forgive me?" Diana questioned through tears.

"The same way he answered the woman caught in adultery. She, too, felt condemned. Men brought her to Jesus to stone her.

They were asking him to agree with their judgment against her, and he forgave her, but he also looked forward to the future and said, 'Go and sin no more.' Neither do I condemn you." Leonab paused a moment and then said, "Something I have learned from God is his ever-enduring patience. He loves you; therefore, he is patient with you."

"Is that from 1 Corinthians 13?" Diana asked.

"What do you mean?" asked Leonab.

"Let me see your Bible." Diana flipped to the passage and handed it back to Leonab. "Read this to me, will you?"

> *And though I bestow all my goods to feed the poor, and though I give my body to be burned, and have not charity, it profiteth me nothing. Charity suffereth long, and is kind; charity envieth not; charity vaunteth not itself, is not puffed up, doth not behave itself unseemly, seeketh not her own, is not easily provoked, thinketh no evil; Rejoiceth not in iniquity, but rejoiceth in the truth; Beareth all things, believeth all things, hopeth all things, endureth all things.*

"Charity is another word for love," Diana explained. "So you can see why Christians believe that it is not the government's responsibility to provide assistance to other people. Can a government love its citizens? I see so much more clearly now. In our fight for freedoms, we have trampled the rights of others. Do my rights extend to the point where they inhibit yours? Love is not about what rights I can keep for myself but rather what sacrifices are necessary to connect us. I'm so sorry, God."

CHAPTER 15

A few moments later, Stew came out of his bedroom and gingerly closed the door. "I figure I'll let Billy sleep as long as he wants. I think he had a long night; they must have solved most of the world's problems. Let's get some breakfast, and then I want to talk to you, Leonab." Looking at them more closely, Stew took note that they had been engaged in some intimate conversation. "Oh, I'm sorry. Have I interrupted you?"

"No," replied Diana immediately. She quickly turned and wiped her eyes. As the three of them walked downstairs, Diana whispered to Leonab, "Please don't tell anyone my secret."

As they ate breakfast, they chatted about Stew's evening. Three more ambulance calls had come in, one robbery with a gunshot victim, one horseback riding accident, and one guy who fell off a ladder at his house just before midnight.

"The gunshot victim is still in critical condition. The horseback rider has two broken ribs and a punctured lung, but he's stable. The guy who fell off the ladder was intoxicated and broke one leg and his collar bone."

After eating, Diana took the breakfast plates and excused herself. Stew led Leonab to the living room and said, "So about yesterday . . ."

"Oh, I have been reading so much," Leonab said excitedly, "I've got so much to tell you!"

Stew held up his hand. "Stop. Before we go chasing your rabbits, I need to know what happened at the hospital yesterday. What did you do to those people?"

"What do you mean?" Leonab asked defensively.

Stew responded, "They were threatening to sue the hospital because some foreign lady practically assaulted them. Once the security guard convinced them to calm down and explained that you don't work for the hospital and had been removed from the premises, they shut that rhetoric down."

"I was only trying to help them. Your system to help hurting people is so inefficient. You make them writhe in pain and suffer while filling out unnecessary information before you will help them. God does not require any of that information, so I called on him to help them."

"God? So now you are claiming that your Great One is God?" Stew asked.

"Oh, yes!" exclaimed Leonab. "That's what I've been trying to tell you! Your Jesus is the Son of the one you call Yahweh, but we call him Yala. Will you let me hear that song you were playing last night?"

Stew took out his cell phone, scrolled through his playlist, and found the song "At Your Name" by Phil Wickham. She asked to listen to it again and again.

At Your name
The mountains shake and crumble . . .

The oceans roar and tumble . . .
The morning breaks in glory . . .
Creation sings Your story . . .
Angels will bow . . .
Your people cry out

"This is the best musical proclamation of Yala's grandeur I have ever heard," Leonab said.

"Okay, so how did you make the connection?" Stew asked.

"It all came together when I read about Gog and Magog," explained Leonab. "You see, those names are the same in my language. We have a similar prophecy."

"Well, if you want to talk about the end times, you'll have to ask Dad—he's our resident authority on Revelation." Stew winked.

"Okay, I will," she responded. "I have not quite finished what you recommended first."

"Wait, how did you wind up reading Revelation and not all of John? No, never mind, that will likely be another wild goose chase; just carry on."

Apparently, people in this time like to pursue rabbits and geese while engaged in serious conversation, thought Leonab. She wasn't sure how well that would work, but as inefficient as they were, it wouldn't surprise her.

"Jesus kept saying 'I am,' and then the God in Revelation, who is apparently his father but also one and the same, says, 'I am the Alpha and Omega.' Then it finally clicked. Jesus is the Word of Life, and that's what it means when he says "I am." He is *life*; he is *being*. He, Yala or Yahweh, is the Word of Life that was in the beginning and created the worlds. Do you see? In our ancient prophecies, God tells his messenger that his name is I AM."

"Wait," Stew interjected. "You mean when God told Moses that his name is I AM, it was really the Word that created life? That is deep. I hadn't put that all together. And you, from one day of reading, tied it up and put a bow on it. So what does that mean for you?"

Just then, the bell rang in the house again. When Stew went to the front door, it was Mayor Anderson again.

"Stew, good to see you. Is your father home?" Mr. Anderson asked.

"I'm coming, Mayor," Mr. Gofson called as he jogged to the door.

"Henry, I'm afraid I need to ask you a favor," Mayor Anderson began. "We've got a crisis on our hands, and only you can help. You see, the mayoral debate is tomorrow. We were going to use the school gym, but since the school administration had planned to decorate it for the Arts and Crafts Festival tomorrow afternoon, the debate had to be scheduled for the morning. We've got local TV and radio programming reserved, and we can't change that."

"I understand," said Mr. Gofson. "That's why we aren't attending. We have our usual church services tomorrow morning."

"That's exactly what we have to talk about. The school gym is a wreck this morning after the seniors pulled a prank last night and destroyed the stadium, supposedly by accident. Given the outwing nature of our educational system, I wouldn't be surprised if this were intentional sabotage of the mayoral debate," the mayor said, visibly agitated.

"How exactly did they manage to destroy the gym?" asked an interested Stew.

"They decided to stack all the spectator stands on the stage and stand them upright. As if that weren't enough, they moved all the stands from the football field in as well. Thankfully, they are only aluminum. The gym stage couldn't handle the weight, and after the stands crashed, the flooring is in ruins. The cost to repair it will probably exceed the expected gross income for the Arts and Crafts Festival."

"So how can we help?" asked Mr. Gofson.

"Ah, I knew I could count on you, Henry," answered Mayor Anderson. "We need to relocate the debate to the church. You were amenable to hosting it there at one point, so I knew you would be willing to rescue the city in her time of need."

"But Mayor Anderson, the debate is scheduled for the same time as our morning services," answered Mr. Gofson.

"Well, you know, God is interested in the outcome of this election, too," said the mayor. "This is obviously an opportunity for God to speak to the community. Besides, I'll let you do the introduction of the moderator. It's really the only option. I mean, we can't change the TV and radio schedule. Surely the Lord's work extends beyond one Sunday's worship service. We've got to preserve the nation God has entrusted to us. Isn't that the duty of a responsible, devoted Christian?"

Mr. Gofson was uncomfortable. "Okay, Mayor Anderson. I suppose we can hold our services after the debate."

"Excellent!" responded the mayor. "I'll meet you at the church around 2:00 this afternoon to get things set up. Make sure you have the banner, and pick up a dozen two-by-fours for a special project, will ya?"

As Mayor Anderson left, Mr. Gofson said to Stew, "I need you and Billy to go pick up the banner. I thought you'd be delivering it to the school, but it looks like our plans have changed. We'll have to take it to the church and hang it there. You'd better grab some lumber as well, I suppose."

I wonder where they will have the Arts and Crafts Festival, Stew thought.

CHAPTER 16

As Stew waited for Billy to get up and moving, he thought about his love for solving mysteries and contemplating hard questions. Why had he not pieced together the facts about Jesus that Leonab had so easily laid out? He read the Bible—once he'd even read it straight through with one of those read-the-Bible-in-a-year plans. How had he missed these simple, yet profound connections?

Then he got distracted with some junk emails on his phone and remembered that question about a professional puzzle solver. "Hey, Siri, what's the word for a professional puzzle or riddle solver?"

"I found this on the web," came the reply. *Is Siri a girl?* wondered Stew. He had once changed the voice to a British guy. *I suppose in the digital world, people are whoever they want to be, like I can create you in my own image. Wait! Did I actually just think that? Am I making myself out to be God?* He looked at these answers on his phone:

Problem solver – *That seems less than magnanimous.*

Cruciverbalist – *Cool word, but it strictly relates to crossword puzzles.*

Enigmatologist – *Studies and writes mathematical word or logical puzzles—maybe that's it.*

Leonab took the departure of Stew as an opportunity to pose her question about Revelation to Mr. Gofson, since according to Stew, he was some sort of expert on the subject matter. "Mr. Gofson, I have a question about the Bible for you."

"What's that? Oh yes, I'd be delighted to entertain a Bible question," he responded.

"I was reading Revelation about a final battle between Gog and Magog and—"

"I see," interrupted Mr. Gofson. "That's very tricky business."

"I'm wondering if your people, Milsap, will be fighting with God's army or with those of Gog and Magog," Leonab said simply.

"Oh, a splendid question, indeed," said a delighted Mr. Gofson. "Now, I have my own theories on the end times, but let me start by saying that most scholars believe that our nation, the United States, as well as most of the Western world will have been conquered or at least be insignificant by that time."

Leonab tried to interrupt, but Mr. Gofson continued on excitedly. "Now, you see, Gog and Magog may represent Soviet countries led by Russia along with the new Babylonian armies led by modern-day Iraq . . . "

While Mr. Gofson was expounding on his end-time, apocalyptic theories, Mrs. Gofson entered. "Excuse me."

"Huh?" said a surprised Mr. Gofson.

"Leonab," Mrs. Gofson continued, "there's no free ride in this house. If you are not out investigating your issues or actively looking for gainful employment, then you can help Diana and Lily with laundry. And for heaven's sake, borrow some clothes from Lily so those can be washed."

As Leonab walked to the stairs, she heard Mr. Gofson say, "Be careful dwelling too much on the revelations. It may require a seminary degree to properly interpret them." Leonab wondered what a seminary degree was.

Diana and Lily assumed Leonab wouldn't know what a washing machine was since she didn't seem to be from this planet, so they had her sort the clothes and linens into groups while they loaded the two washers. Certainly the six—now seven—people in this house generated a significant amount of dirty laundry, but Mrs. Gofson also ran a laundry service out of her home. There was always laundry in various stages in the other rooms upstairs. Some needed to be washed, others folded, and others ironed and hung. Today was a light load since it was Saturday. Generally, the large loads came in on Monday.

After the last two loads were separated, Diana showed Leonab how to fold. Lily began ironing, and Diana joined her.

While Diana and Lily were ironing in the other room, Leonab began thinking about the betrayal of Jesus and his subsequent arrest. *Where will Jesus go to raise an army for the battle between Gog and Magog? Wait! He couldn't be preparing at his time for a battle that doesn't happen until after the present time. Well, where is he going? Jesus gets wounded somewhere in the past, though, because his blood has to be our redemption. In the end, Jesus has to win this particular battle so he can fight the future battle.*

But why did Jesus say that Peter couldn't go with him without dying? Maybe he is going to a battle, but it will have weapons far superior to Peter's sword. Does Jesus have guns like the people in this time?

Lily stepped in and interrupted Leonab's thoughts. "Thanks for not imposing on our conversation last night."

"Oh, I could see you were working through hurt feelings and misunderstandings. It wasn't my place to intrude."

"You're really a unique person, you know that? You ask questions and listen carefully before giving opinions that are reasonably well formed but appear to be free from personal bias. It's as if you don't have a personal interest in the result. For some reason, though, it seems like you are always a contrarian," Lily said, offering for the first time something of a compliment.

"Well, I'm not from here, so I'm not familiar with your customs or the issues you face here and now. And since this is not my place in t—" Leonab caught herself. "—the world, I am not affected by these issues. When we are in need of counsel, we should seek out unbiased advisors who are not directly affected by the outcome in order to avoid a conflict of personal interest. At the same time, though, it is important for an advisor to clearly hear both sides of any argument. Without a balanced understanding, how can one come to a reasonable conclusion?"

"Exactly! I know that I struggle listening to opposing views because I feel so passionately against them, but when I feel sympathetic to an opposing argument, I find myself getting angry. As for the Gofsons, I don't think they can even spell tolerance."

"What do you mean?" asked Leonab.

"They are just so judgmental. You heard them," retorted Lily. "They don't even pretend to hear opposing views."

"Tolerance suggests that in the midst of two strongly opposing views, the parties agree to disagree," Leonab said. "Have they not agreed to house you here in spite of your opposing views?"

"Well, yeah, but they won't agree that the government should help take care of the poor, for instance, and that's a basic human right, isn't it?" Lily responded.

"It sounds like," challenged Leonab, "what you are seeking is their approval or that they agree and submit to your view. Ironically, you are not being tolerant of them in their own home."

"What?" exclaimed Lily. "Siri, what is the definition of tolerance?"

Leonab watched as Lily asked this of her cell phone. *Who's Siri?* she wondered. Then came the reply from the cell phone: "The ability or willingness to tolerate something; in particular, the existence of opinions or behavior that one does not necessarily agree with."

"Why do they always include a variation of the word in the definition?" moaned Lily. "Now we'll have to look up *tolerate*. Let's just use the dictionary app."

"That does seem inefficient," commented Leonab.

"Here it is," said Lily. "'Tolerate: to allow to be or to be done without prohibition, hindrance, or contradiction; to put up with.'* See, they are not allowing the government to provide for the poor and needy, so they are not tolerant of my beliefs at all." As Lily was speaking, Diana walked in.

"Tolerating someone's beliefs is different from enacting policies enforcing those beliefs," responded Leonab. "Are you asking others to enact your policies or tolerate your beliefs? It seems that the Gofsons are very tolerant of your beliefs because

---

*"tolerate," Merriam-Webster, https://www.merriam-webster.com/dictionary/tolerate.

they put up with them and do not prohibit or hinder you from having them. To tolerate your policies, however, both their own policies and yours must conflict and be active. It sounds as if you want to impose your policies without following your own government-prescribed protocol to put them into practice. And since this has not occurred, you accuse others of not being tolerant of your beliefs. That is transference. You have transferred the frustration you feel toward not having a majority to support your own personal agenda to an unfounded complaint that others are not tolerant of your beliefs. That complaint would be legitimate if others did not allow you to hold your beliefs."

As Diana and Lily were thinking on this, Leonab continued. "If the Gofsons were truly not tolerant of your beliefs, they would kick you out of their house, or in the extreme, they would kill you. Yet here you are. For you to insist they agree with your views and implement policies without due process is not tolerant on your part because you are not allowing them to have beliefs that contradict your own."

"Um," stammered Lily, "I'll have to think about that. I don't think you understand what I'm saying at all."

Diana, who had been quietly introspective throughout this conversation, spoke up. "I think she's right, Lily. We have been somewhat ungrateful to the Gofsons."

"Yeah, but they're high-horse, soap-box bigots," Lily responded angrily.

"I'll agree they are insensitive, just as you have been on occasion, like that comment to Billy last night. But even if they were bigots, we are responsible for our own behavior, not theirs. Do you want to go so far as to say that the government should be responsible for our behavior, in which case the government would also have to be responsible for their behavior?" Diana responded.

"Whatever." Lily brushed off the conversation. "Hey, I'm getting hungry. It's noon. Can we grab some lunch and finish the laundry afterward?"

"We're just about done," said Diana. "Let's finish up first. It won't take us 15 minutes."

"All right," conceded Lily.

CHAPTER 17

Stew and Billy had already returned from their errand and were eating sandwiches while waiting for Mr. Gofson. While the girls made sandwiches, Lily asked Billy, "Where were you two while we did all the laundry?"

"We went down to the lumberyard and the sign shop on Pearl Street to pick up some things for the mayoral debate," Billy said. "It's going to be held at the church tomorrow morning."

Diana was confused. "I thought it was being held at the high school gym."

"Well," Stew responded, "that was the plan until this morning when Mayor Anderson told us the gym was out of commission. Since in the past Dad was willing to hold the debate at the church during the afternoon, Mr. Anderson felt no remorse in imposing and encroaching on Sunday morning services. Originally, the school was a more favorable location than the church because the school was viewed as more of a neutral territory."

"What do you mean by neutral territory?" questioned Leonab. "Is there a war going on?"

"Good Lord!" exclaimed Lily. "Where have you been all your life? Haven't you even seen the conflicts around you? We've told you about the opposing views on various issues, and you somehow seem to quickly assess and easily propose counterarguments," she sneered.

"Yes, but those issues, while involved and conditional, are fairly clear once you take your own desires out of the evaluation and think about the good of the community," Leonab responded. "The issues would not lead you to fight if people would lay aside their own selfish agendas and think about the impacts their choices have on those around them rather than how they will benefit from them."

"Yeah, well, here we are," Lily said, exasperated. "We're basically two groups. On the one hand, you have the in-wingers who are Bible-thumpers who believe personal freedoms should be suppressed." She gestured on her fingers as she enumerated. "Those such as one, a woman's right to decide about whether or not she wants to have a baby, two, a person's right to end his or her own life, three, a person's right to choose his or her own identity, and four, whether a person loves a man, a woman, a child, or any combination. They also irrationally believe we should all carry guns and that poor people should be abandoned in the streets and left to scavenge for food from charities while rich people horde their wealth and don't share or only share on their own terms."

She paused to take a breath and then animatedly continued. "On the other hand, you have the out-wingers who value individuals' rights and freedoms to choose what happens to their own bodies, to choose when and how to die if they are facing certain near-term death, to choose how to express themselves based on their own feelings, and to love whomever and however they want. They also want to protect humanity from the danger of every Tom, Dick, Harry, or Smith & Wesson who wants to carry a gun, while requiring individual high-earners to take care of others in the community."

Lily took another breath and then added, "Never mind the fact that the in-wingers have historically been closed-minded and oppressive to women, Black people, and anyone else who isn't their version of normal. Surely when you understand all these points, you can see that the out-wingers are clear moral superiors. It's absolutely crazy anyone could agree with those in-wingers, right?"

After a brief pause, Diana said quietly, "While we basically have these two groups, there are ranges within each one. For instance, the radical in-wingers are called wing-nuts, and they represent the loudest voices on that side. The extreme out-wingers are called far-outs, and they are the loudest voices on that side."

Diana looked at Lily and then added, "What Lily said about the in-wingers historically being oppressive is mostly true, but the wing-nuts are primarily responsible for that. You know that's true, right, Lily? Some of the Bible-thumpers may have been involved, but many of them were opposed to it. Perhaps now the far-outs have swung the pendulum too far the other way."

Leonab was confused momentarily about the swinging pendulum, but she asked, "What about people who agree with points on both sides?"

Stew responded, "Between the two groups, there are a few voices of reason in a crossover; they are called swingers."

Leonab thought about the whole description and then concluded, "Your society is so self-contradicting. Within each of these groups, the values are inconsistent . . . "

She was interrupted by Mr. Gofson who walked in from outside and called for Stew and Billy to help him haul the materials to the church to set up for the mayoral debate.

CHAPTER 18

After the boys left the table and joined Mr. Gofson to head to the church, Lily looked at Leonab and said, "You are a piece of work, you know that? Come on, Diana, let's go for a walk."

Diana shrugged at Leonab and followed her friend out of the room and the house. Finding herself alone again, Leonab went back upstairs to find the Bible. She opened it where she had left off and began reading and questioning.

Jesus is on trial now? she wondered. *What is this? Why do the people reject him after he's done so many things for them? They're asking for a robber to be released instead of him? What is going on? Jesus is being beaten?*

How could Yala let himself or his Son be beaten like this? I would never let this happen to Bontaq. Surely this could not be happening. If you find no fault in him, why did you have him beaten? She read on.

> *Then delivered he him therefore unto them to be crucified. And they took Jesus, and led him away. And he bearing his cross went forth into a place called the place of a skull, which is called in the Hebrew Golgotha: Where they crucified him, and two other with him, on either side one, and Jesus in the midst.*

As Leonab read these words, her eyes filled with tears. *How could Yala let his Son die like this? Especially considering the shame, the misery, and the suffering?*

> *. . . he said, It is finished: and he bowed his head, and gave up the ghost.*

Jesus is dead? Can Yala really die? Why did he say, "It is finished," here? Doesn't Jesus say something like that after the last battle?

> *For these things were done, that the scripture should be fulfilled, a bone of him shall not be broken. And again another scripture saith, They shall look on him whom they pierced.*

When she read this, she halted. Hadn't she read some prophecy like these words? Could the scriptures referred to here also be the words of the prophets she had read in her own language? *Who is this Nicodemus? It is that weird name mentioned before when I skipped a portion. I will return to that segment after I finish this since there are only two more pages*, she thought.

This is confusing—why is the stone rolled away? What? Jesus isn't dead? That's unbelievable. Oh, apparently Thomas agrees with me.

Then saith he to Thomas, Reach hither thy finger, and behold my hands; and reach hither thy hand, and thrust it into my side: and be not faithless, but believing. And Thomas answered and said unto him, My LORD and my God. Jesus saith unto him, Thomas, because thou hast seen me, thou hast believed: blessed are they that have not seen, and yet have believed. And many other signs truly did Jesus in the presence of his disciples, which are not written in this book: But these are written, that ye might believe that Jesus is the Christ, the Son of God; and that believing ye might have life through his name.

"Yala, I do believe!" she enthused. "I do love you; I will follow you." Then, remembering Nicodemus, she flipped back to the first chapter and started skimming for his name. *Here is that confusing comment about being born again.*

For God so loved the world, that he gave his only begotten Son, that whosoever believeth in him should not perish, but have everlasting life. For God sent not his Son into the world to condemn the world; but that the world through him might be saved. He that believeth on him is not condemned: but he that believeth not is condemned already, because he hath not believed in the name of the only begotten Son of God. And this is the condemnation, that light is come into the world, and men loved darkness rather than light, because their deeds were evil.

Now I see it, she thought. *Jesus came to rescue the condemned.* Even in her recollection of the prophecies she had read in her own language, which were referenced here, she understood that humans were innately selfish. *This same truth,* she thought, *is echoed through the values of the two political groups. The in-wingers want to prohibit abortion because it is a selfish decision devaluing life that negatively impacts society, while the out-wingers want to prohibit gun ownership because of their demonstrated potential of taking the lives of others. Both groups seem to agree that people are naturally bad, and therefore sin must be natural. Jesus came to die to remove that sin just as a lamb was sacrificed in the scriptures I have read from the prophets.*

When Mr. Gofson drove up to the church, Stew and Billy got out and started unloading the materials. While they were hauling all the lumber and the banner into the church, Mayor Anderson arrived and joined them in the church sanctuary. "Okay, Henry," he said, "let's get to work. The first thing we need to do is build a railing down the center of the church."

Mr. Gofson was confused for a moment. "You mean you want to build a barrier to separate the citizens of the community from each other, depending on what political group they are in?"

"It's for the safety of the community as well as to preserve the church property," the mayor responded. "Just imagine what the extremists will do if they get into a heated debate. They'll start throwing punches. I think it's critical to keep the voters divided for their own sake and for the sake of democracy and civility."

"That seems like a contradiction," said Stew. "Don't the people of the community have to come together to talk through issues in order to work toward the common good? At the very least, we are all on common ground when we cast our ballots."

"Now listen here, son," said the mayor. "I've been in politics a long time, and in my career, I've seen everything from yo-mammas to physical mudslinging to drunken brawls. When I tell you this is a crucial component of this debate, I'm not exaggerating."

"Stew," Mr. Gofson said, "you and Billy get to working on that railing. It will be okay. We will take it down before the service."

Once they had finished installing the central banister separating the church into halves, Mayor Anderson directed them to put up the banner. "It's going to go right behind the podium; that way it will be viewed prominently on TV."

"Dad," Stew began, "won't that hide the cross and the baptistery behind the banner?"

"Son, it's not a big deal. The mayoral debate is only going to occur this one time," Mr. Gofson responded.

"It's not like the baptistery gets used all that often," snickered Billy just loud enough that only Stew could hear him.

CHAPTER 19

When the boys got back from the church, Mrs. Gofson was in the kitchen preparing dinner. Leonab had been too engaged in her reading to overhear the front porch conversations between Lily and Diana over the past hour after they returned from their walk. When Mrs. Gofson heard the door open, she went and saw the five of them come in. "And what have you done with Leonab?" she asked.

"Maybe she's upstairs taking a nap," replied Diana, and quickly raced up the stairs to find Leonab. She found Leonab weeping on the floor, with the Bible on the bed open to the book of Philippians. Apparently, she'd been reading the Bible all afternoon. *Good words in there by Paul*, Diana thought, but she usually focused on the Gospels and the love chapter. "Here," she called to Leonab as she pitched her clean clothes to her. "Put these back on and wash up. We gotta get down to supper."

"But, Diana," replied Leonab, "I have so much to share with you now."

"No, not now. Later. Right now, we have to get down to dinner—pronto," Diana said, practically dragging Leonab to the restroom to help her wash her face. Once Leonab was in control of herself again, Diana told her that the boys were back and Mrs. Gofson was setting the table.

As the two hurried downstairs, they saw the table set and everyone waiting for them. Once Diana and Leonab sat down, they all joined hands as had been their practice. Mr. Gofson prayed, "Lord, we thank thee for the hands thou hast given us to work and the bread thou hast provided for us to eat. Amen."

Do we work for what God provides? thought Leonab. *Didn't I just read that we are saved by grace through faith and not by our own works?*

Before Leonab could verbalize this question, Mrs. Gofson asked about the preparations for the mayoral debate. Mr. Gofson described the mayor's concern for the sanctuary and about Billy and Stew building the banister down the middle of the sanctuary. "We have to be at the church bright and early tomorrow, dear," he said. "The TV crew and the radio techs need to bring in and set up all their equipment. They'll want to view angles and set up their own microphones. Mayor Anderson invited me to introduce the Police Chief as the moderator of the debate. I asked if I could give an invocation, but he said that would be inappropriate as it may make some of the attendees uncomfortable."

Stew said, "It seems to me like we are bending over backward to help him out. I'm not sure he's as devoted to God as he is to politics, Dad."

"Nonsense, son," Mr. Gofson replied. "He's been a member of the church for nearly as long as you've been alive. He's just particular about how we should interact with voters. After all, God cares about our election process, and we don't want people to see the church as a hostile environment. The church needs to be a place where people feel welcomed, doesn't it?"

At this comment, Lily asked politely to be excused, and she was quickly followed by Billy and Diana. Leonab could see her questions and message were getting nowhere at the table, so she also asked to be excused. Stew got up quickly, saying he had to get to bed for his early morning shift.

Leonab tried to engage him in conversation again, but he said they would have plenty of time Monday. "Perhaps we'll even play some more cards. I'll let you play while I coach you," he said.

At the top of the stairs, Stew went to the boys' bedroom door to the right as he said good night to the other three who were sitting at the card table. Leonab slowly approached the table and sat down, uninvited. Conversation had all but ceased abruptly when she and Stew appeared at the top of the stairs. They stared at her. She looked back at them. *Woe is me,* she thought, *for I am one of brokenness, and I dwell with people of immense brokenness.* No one spoke.

She thought of her interactions with each of these three and noted their individual struggles. *In spite of these hardships, these three have a passion for life, but they don't seem to know the path. Stew, at least, has found the path, but is he too busy to embrace it? The Gofsons clearly know some of God's words, but they seem swayed by political interests. Then there is Mayor Anderson, who is clearly interested in building his own kingdom rather than that of Yahweh. Brokenness—will the blind lead the blind?*

"You've almost persuaded me to listen to you, Leonab," Lily said. "But tonight I want to think through more of your logic. I'll be ready to talk with you again tomorrow."

As Lily got up and went to the girls' bedroom, Billy also stood. "Well, I'm tired from a short night and hard work. I'll see y'all tomorrow."

Diana sat still and stared off into space for a moment longer before asking, "Will you tell me more about your TVs and how you use them?"

After a moment, Leonab said, "Look at that teevee over there. What do you see?"

"I see a reflection of the light bulb, the wall, and the ceiling. I suppose if I got closer, it would be like a mirror," Diana replied.

"But the teevee screen, unlike the mirror, is dark and blank. When you see yourself in the reflection from this teevee, think of the futility of your own struggles." Leonab paused. "As individuals, we are all broken. Our souls are dark and empty just like that teevee screen. The pictures I have observed on your teevees serve to prove this, as the scenes of chaos and destruction reflect the anger and division among the people. Even the members of this house are conflicted and plagued with their own inconsistencies, contradictions, and sin."

She continued, "This brokenness is what we see. While your teevees serve to entertain you and distract you with that information, our blank teevee screens show us this same message without the distraction or the images. In the blankness and emptiness, we see the brokenness, but we also see hope. In the stillness, there is peace. You see, darkness and blankness are not always bad. They represent an empty canvas. In our sacred writings, historians recorded that God took the dark, empty canvas and created beauty and life. The emptiness can also represent a new beginning."

"Wow," said Diana, a tear forming at the inside corner of her eye. "That is beautiful. We don't see darkness or emptiness like that at all. We see them as scary or boring at best, but you're right. The Bible says that in the beginning, God created the heaven and the earth, and while the earth was empty, his Spirit moved while he spoke things into existence."

"That is what our sacred scriptures tell us, too," said Leonab. "But you have pieces we have lost or otherwise do not have. John wrote that the Word of God was in the beginning, created all things, and was the light of men. This light is Jesus, and while he comes to create and bring light and life to the darkness, we don't comprehend it. We reject it."

Leonab gathered her thoughts. "In fact, according to your Bible, the darkness of humankind led us to crucify Jesus, and then there was only darkness because we had killed the light. But that was only the first time Jesus said the words 'It is finished.' I was so confused about this because he is prophesied to say similar words after the last battle between Gog and Magog. It didn't make any sense that Jesus could have died. Then as I read on, Jesus, the light, overcame the darkness of death. He's alive! He took the darkness and emptiness of the grave and created new life. That is the hope my people look forward to in the emptiness we see in our teevees."

Leonab had gotten so excited she could hardly stand it. "You see, when Jesus fought that first battle of the war in John, he was looking forward to his first victory—overcoming the grave. Since the hard part of suffering was done, he proclaimed, 'It is finished.' But he lives to repeat those words in a time beyond yours and mine when he wins the second battle. This first battle was for the souls of men and women, his beloved subjects and the sheep of his pasture. But the second battle is for his kingdom or his territory, the rest of creation as he later creates a new heaven and a new earth.

"Jesus died for his enemies, the very people who killed him," Leonab continued, "who, really, considering our own brokenness, is your people and mine, Diana. But there's hope for the future. Jesus is alive."

"How do I get this hope, Leonab?" Diana asked, now in tears.

"It is easy, and it is hard," answered Leonab. "Your scriptures tell us that whoever calls on the name of the Lord will be saved. It says if you confess with your mouth that Jesus is Lord and believe in your heart that God raised him from the dead, you will be saved. For with the heart we believe unto righteousness; and with the mouth confession is made for salvation.

"But I'm pretty sure that the word *believe* implies much more than these words and knowledge," Leonab said. "According to the rest of what I've been reading in the Bible and based on what I know of Yala through our sacred scriptures, belief and faith are demonstrated by action. If we truly believe, then we will study Jesus's character, learn to value what he values, and live the way he lived," Leonab clarified. "It is complicated because we are saved by grace through faith, not by works that we perform. But somehow, that faith that we claim is expressed in what we do, the choices we make, and the way we treat others.

"When we see Jesus in his glory willingly humbling himself, submitting to God's plan, we can better understand the character traits God values," Leonab added as she remembered the words she had most recently been reading. She recalled one passage that said something like this: "Let this mind be in you that was also in Christ Jesus, who made himself a nobody and took on the form of a servant and humbled himself to die, even to die on the cross."

"Do you know," continued Leonab, "that my scriptures state that anyone who is hung on a tree is cursed? But the same God who said that hung on a tree for us. Jesus took the curse for us. He valued you enough to submit all his own comforts and rights to reconcile you, his enemy, from death. If he was willing to do this for you, should you not do the same for others? God values people above all else. That is why he fought that battle first. He will fight a second battle at a later time to redeem the rest of creation. So it is our job to follow his battle cry for the souls of the enemies he loves—regardless of how we feel about them, regardless of how they treat us. We must submit our own comforts, rights, and desires to reconcile others to Jesus."

Diana began weeping uncontrollably, and Leonab stood behind her with hands on her shoulders, praying. "Now I believe; I really get it," Diana said. They embraced.

When they walked into the bedroom, they found Lily pondering alone on her bed. She saw their tears in stark contrast to their smiling faces, and though her heart melted, she turned away and said, "Good night."

CHAPTER 20

Peaceful sleep came easily to Leonab. She'd found the firm content of the message, and she knew the people of Milsap needed to hear it. She just needed to figure out how to deliver it. She figured she would talk to Stew on Monday afternoon about going back to the hospital. *Maybe he has determined with whom I should speak,* she thought. *In the meantime, I hope Lily will open up tomorrow afternoon.*

She woke when she heard movement in the large room and went to find Stew putting on his shoes to start his shift at the ER. "Sorry I woke you," he apologized.

Another sentence with no subject. It is also not an imperative with an understood subject. It must be an example of how the people of Milsap are unwilling to accept responsibility for their own actions. Leonab put that thought out of her mind and said, "I am ready to go to the hospital and share my message now. Have you determined who will be able to help me?"

"Look," said Stew, "I understand how important this is to you, but I'm running late right now. We can talk about it tomorrow, okay?"

As Stew drove to the hospital, he thought about the song he and Leonab had listened to together—*how long ago was that?* He thought he was accustomed to this type of work schedule, but for some reason, his rhythm was off, maybe because he had switched shifts. He hoped to switch back next month. He needed to give Lou a call later to pose the question or at least plant the idea.

When he got to the hospital, he followed his normal check-in routine, but as he passed the chair where he'd left Leonab reading the Bible, he noticed the New Testament had a paper crammed into it. He picked it up and saw that it was John, chapter 8. *This must be where she left off before assaulting those patients. What did she do, anyway?* As he looked at the Bible, he read these words:

> Jesus replied, "Very truly I tell you, everyone who sins
> is a slave to sin. Now a slave has no permanent place
> in the family, but a son belongs to it forever. So if the
> Son sets you free, you will be free indeed."

Am I the servant of sin? he thought. Everything that Leonab had said was so clear and coherent. Did she have some special knowledge he didn't have? *Impossible! She'd never even seen a Bible until I loaned her this one. Why does she talk as if she knows the future? Maybe she's mad. It's plausible. There's a fine line between genius and lunatic.*

Stew wondered what it meant to be free like what Jesus was promising here. He was a Christian, sure; he'd walked the aisle of the church long ago—nearly 30 years ago. What Leonab had talked about, though, had awakened in him that passion he used to have. But it seemed like life kept getting in the way; he was too busy to pursue spiritual things. *No, I'm not too busy, I just have to make time to do what is important.* He resolved then and there to spend Monday hearing Leonab out and studying the Bible with her. *Then,* he thought, *I can determine if she needs special help and how I can return to faithful Christian service.* He knew he would face challenges with his parents and with his friends, but he was confident he'd found the right path.

CHAPTER 21

Sunday morning was a blur of activity downstairs. Breakfast was an afterthought. There was coffee, but Mr. and Mrs. Gofson were busy changing and rechanging clothes, applying face paint, washing it off, and reapplying it. Billy and Lily were talking upstairs while Diana was getting dressed. Leonab was alone downstairs, only partially aware of the chaos surrounding her. When they were finally done, Mr. and Mrs. Gofson called for them all to get in the vehicles for immediate departure.

When they got to the church, Leonab could see Stew's and Billy's handiwork in the fresh lumber crafted into the central banister dividing the church into two sides. She looked up and saw a huge banner announcing "Milsap Mayoral Debate." She had hardly taken all this in when a tremendous entourage of people came in with such a commotion that the enormous banner quaked.

Leonab thought about the dividing rail. *Does the battle between these political opponents really warrant a special railing to separate them? If people cannot get together, then they will never learn to agree.*

Diana approached her. "I talked with Lily this morning, and I think she's willing to hear you out this afternoon. It's interesting, you know. She and I are very different, and you have addressed us just like Jesus addressed Martha and Mary. You challenge Lily, and you cry with me. But your ultimate goal has been to show both of us love. Thank you, Leonab."

There's that verb with no subject again. You can't save them all, she thought. *I must choose to focus on truth rather than my personal preferences.* "It is God who is at work within me to accomplish his goals and express his love. It is not about me."

CHAPTER 22

The sanctuary began filling up quickly. Mr. and Mrs. Gofson had specially reserved seats on the side of the stage. Mayor Anderson was to be seated next to them— no surprise there. All three were busy mingling at the front with well-dressed people but noticeably only those on their side of the barrier.

Leonab joined Lily, Diana, and Billy, who were sitting halfway to the back next to the central railing but on the opposite side of the railing from the Gofsons. Leonab thought about where she had sat in the ER. *Being on the outside looking in is different than being on the inside looking in. What difference does it make where I sit? What really matters is where I stand. Both of these groups have issues that prohibit them from seeing and accepting God's future.* At some point, she would share the truth with someone who could communicate that message to the rest of these people.

As ushers began to quiet the crowd, Mayor Anderson pushed Mr. Gofson up to the pulpit to begin. As Mr. Gofson welcomed the guests, he said, "Friends, family, fellow citizens of our great city of Milsap, I am Mr. Gofson, pastor of First Jesus Church of Milsap, and I have the distinguished honor of inviting you to the Milsap Mayoral Debate. Also, welcome to those of you joining us on television and those who are joining us on the radio."

"Get to the point, old man," jeered one young man sitting seven rows directly in front of Leonab.

"Yes, well, without further ado, I would like to introduce the moderator for today's debate, Chief of Police Richard Crondell," Mr. Gofson said.

As the applause rose from the crowd, recognition dawned on Leonab as she remembered that this was the man who'd sent her to the hospital.

"Welcome, all," began the Police Chief. "Today, this event is scheduled for us to hear about and influence the future of Milsap as well as her inhabitants. This is not about your personal agenda or your grievances. I urge you to respect the rules of civility as members of our beloved Milsap, as well as to honor this sacred place, whether or not you agree with the beliefs held and encouraged herein."

"Thank you," said Mr. Gofson from his seat.

The Police Chief continued, disregarding this comment. "Remember, no matter who you are, your color, creed, gender, or beliefs, you must hold others in high regard and respect them as you also wish to be respected. How you treat those who differ with you on your principles will have more of an impact on the future of Milsap than who our next mayor will be."

This comment produced some rumblings, but there was applause as well. The Police Chief then announced that the debate would kick off with a two-minute introduction from each candidate and then would proceed with questions and answers. The first question would be selected from a group of previously submitted and approved questions, and then the floor microphones would be opened, alternating questions from side to side.

"We will begin with a coin toss to determine which candidate will offer his or her introduction first. After the introductions and follow-ups, we will alternate which candidate answers questions first. In order to determine who will call the coin toss, I have selected a number between zero and 100. That number has been sealed in this envelope." The Police Chief was holding an envelope high in the air. "The candidates are kindly requested to write down a number on the cardstock paper on their tables."

The Police Chief took out a coin and tossed it several times, practicing. Once each candidate had written down a number, Police Chief Crondell asked them to call out their numbers. Mrs. Albright, representing the in-wing group, had chosen 24, and Mr. Ludlow, representing the out-wing group, had chosen 73. The number on the sealed envelope was 64, so Mr. Ludlow called heads for the coin toss. "Let the candidates take note," called the Police Chief, "that the coin has fallen tails. Therefore, Mrs. Albright will give her opening two-minute speech first."

Before Mrs. Albright could open her mouth, toward the back of the room on Leonab's side of the sanctuary was a faint chant of "Not my mayor, not my mayor" growing in intensity. The Police Chief cleared his throat into the microphone and looked in that direction. Rather than give the disruption merit, Mrs. Albright addressed the crowd in a clear, crisp voice. "Fellow citizens of Milsap, I am honored to be here today seeking your support to lead our city to become great again. We have seen a decline in our economy and in our community over the past 20 years, though our current mayor has been working to rectify these circumstances. We have seen division building among various segments and subgroups of our population. I am here to remind you that we are one people with varying values and interests, not various people groups at war with one another over the things we value. If elected to serve as your mayor, I will work to restore unity to our city so all citizens have the same rights regardless of creed, color, or socioeconomic background. It is the mayor's responsibility, alongside the city council, to protect this community from threats to our economy, culture, and moral standards. I will fight to preserve the constitutional rights of every citizen—"

"Time," called out the Police Chief.

"—to ensure that every corner of Milsap receives equal opportunity," continued Mrs. Albright.

"Time," called the Police Chief again in a firm voice. "This is a warning, Madam Albright."

There was murmuring on both sides of the aisle. Applause had broken out periodically during the speech from the other side of the sanctuary, so Leonab couldn't hear everything, but all in all, she thought Mrs. Albright sounded like a reasonably good government official. The Police Chief then invited Mr. Ludlow to give his introduction.

As Mr. Ludlow prepared to speak, a few cheers erupted from the same people who had chanted against Mrs. Albright. The out-wing candidate waved and smiled. "Friends, we have come to a pivotal point in the history of our beloved Milsap—a time when decisions must be made about the future. Never before in the history of humankind have we faced the pace of evolution we are seeing today—the evolution of technology, of education, of human thought, of society, and of relationships. We have to make decisions today that will have long-lasting and far-reaching impacts on our future, the future of our children, and the people who will follow in our footsteps. We must decide whether we will digress to some former glory that existed in a previous time where we faced different circumstances and had less access to real-time information, where we knew less about human psychology and physiology, and where we knew less about our environment, or whether we will progress to a new and greater glory taking full advantage of all we have learned. We are not the same generation as our parents or grandparents, so why should we settle for their beliefs and institutions? Look around you—"

"Time," called out the Police Chief.

"—The world is changing. Will we change with it or be left behind?" finished Mr. Ludlow.

"Time. This is a warning to both candidates," charged the Police Chief. "We must respect the boundaries of our own current institution to give our citizens a fair representation of who each of you is and what each of you stands for. If you do not respect the time, you are also disrespecting these, your fellow citizens and potential constituents."

There had been more cheers and applause during this speech from Leonab's side of the room. What she heard about effecting change for the future seemed really positive. It was as if both candidates were passionate about working to improve life in Milsap.

CHAPTER 23

"Now we will proceed to the question-and-answer period," the Police Chief said. "Mr. Ludlow, you will have the first opportunity to respond. You will have one minute and 30 seconds; then Mrs. Albright will have the same amount of time. After each candidate has spoken, you will each have two opportunities to offer 30-second rebuttals. Is that understood?"

When both candidates agreed, Police Chief Crondell held up another envelope, this one larger than the first, and said, "In this envelope is a single question selected at random from 10 questions presented and approved by the city council. The question is, 'What will you do as mayor to address the widening pay and wealth gap among the various groups within our citizenry?' Mr. Ludlow, you have one minute and 30 seconds."

"The widening pay and wealth gap has been a growing problem in the long term, over decades," Mr. Ludlow answered. "One of the primary ways to address this issue in the long term is to make education available to young people of low socioeconomic status. I'm not talking about affordable education. There's no such thing. If education is going to be a priority for the next generation, then we must make it truly affordable, as in free. It's time that we, the city, invest in our future. How will we pay for it? We must raise taxes on the businesses here in our city. They have been benefiting from us, the citizens, for years, and it is time for them to start giving back. I will institute the Scholarship Tax. Furthermore, this gap must be addressed in the short term, as well. By immediately raising the minimum wage to a living wage—"

"Time," called out the Police Chief.

"—at which," Mr. Ludlow attempted to continue.

"Mr. Ludlow," the Police Chief warned. "Madam Albright?"

Mrs. Albright had prepared for this question. "I wholeheartedly agree with my opposition on two points. First, the widening pay and wealth gap is a long-term problem. But being a long-term problem, it cannot be resolved overnight as Mr. Ludlow would suggest. His radical attack on local businesses will only serve to undermine the very economic system we are attempting to correct. We must slowly encourage companies to correct their compensation policies. Doing so immediately would have catastrophic effects on them. Second, education is the key to the long-term, full correction of the issue. We must make education opportunities more available to all, not just low-income groups, and we must seek logical means to secure those benefits. The primary responsibility of a business is to be profitable, not to educate. That's the responsibility of families and society as a whole. We must seek alternate avenues, perhaps establishing charity-funded scholarships, apprenticeships, or journeymanships. College is not—"

"Time," called out the Police Chief.

" —for everyone," finished Mrs. Albright.

After giving a stern look to Madam Albright, the Police Chief turned to Mr. Ludlow and said, "Mr. Ludlow, you have 30 seconds to rebut."

"Madam Albright lives in a world of unicorns and rainbows," Mr. Ludlow jumped in. "Charitably funded scholarships don't work because big corporations that generate enormous profits will not voluntarily give back to do their part as members of society to promote education. We must forcibly take from the super-wealthy and give to the rest of society."

"Time," called the Police Chief. "Madam Albright, 30 seconds."

"Mr. Ludlow claims to desire to promote equality, and yet he continues to dwell on and create divisions between the haves and the have-nots. Overtaxing and penalizing our businesses will cripple their ability to return investors' money, lead to layoffs, and hurt our economy in the long term."

"Time," said the Police Chief. When Mrs. Albright didn't attempt to add or finish, he said, "Very good. Now, Mr. Ludlow, final rebuttal."

"This idea of trickle-down economics is complete nonsense," Mr. Ludlow argued. "Corporate profits are at an all-time high. Our local businesses must give back, and it must begin now. Besides this, Mrs. Albright knows that I want us all to be equal, and that is precisely why I must continue to point out that we are not. It's the—"

"Time," called out Police Chief Crondell. "Madam Albright, 30 seconds."

"By constantly pointing out the differences and continually insisting on preferential treatment, Mr. Ludlow is exacerbating the issues I am trying to resolve by promoting equal rights for all and equal accountability for all. Furthermore, since your paychecks are drawn from local companies, they are giving back to the community every time you cash your—"

"Time," called out the Police Chief.

"—paychecks," finished Madam Albright unapologetically.

"We will now entertain questions from the floor," announced Police Chief Crondell.

CHAPTER 24

During the first dispute period, various people had lined up at the public microphones on both sides of the room. Questions came from the floor on alternating sides, and discussion followed a pattern similar to the discussions Leonab had experienced with Lily and Diana—abortion, gun rights, same-sex marriage, legalization of drugs.

While both sides were animated, expressing approval and disapproval of Mrs. Abright's most recent comment, Leonab decided this might be her best opportunity to get her message to the people of Milsap. While the crowd was still jeering, she sneaked past the line of would-be inquisitors and got to the microphone just as the Police Chief was ready to recognize her for a question. There was a commotion of disagreement as the lady displaced in line caused a stir, but in the end, Leonab won the mic.

As soon as her microphone was on, Leonab said, "Do you not realize that each of you has self-contradictory positions?"

As soon as Mayor Anderson heard her voice, he stood, calling out to her, "You are a guest here, and—"

He didn't get to finish that thought because, as he was speaking, the enormous banner fell, and one of the wooden dowels hit him just under his right eye with enough force to knock him out. Mr. Gofson, who was close by but far enough away to avoid injury, immediately knelt to check on him. The Police Chief rushed over, as well. The commotion onstage drew all eyes in the room as well as every TV spectator. Those listening on the radio, including Stew, were left wondering what had happened. Sally at the ER front desk radioed Stew immediately. On TV, it was unclear who had been hit by the falling object, and she thought Stew would want to go check on his father.

All eyes were on the small crowd around the unconscious mayor—all eyes except Leonab's because she had finally seen it. Above the podium, hidden behind the banner and now revealed to the sanctuary, was a white cross over a field of red crimson. It was some sort of round, transparent glass. Leonab could see that there was a light behind it to draw the audience's attention to it.

Taking advantage of the disturbance, she jumped onto the stage and took the Police Chief's place at the podium. Though this caused more unrest, Leonab turned to the Police Chief and asked, "Police Chief Richard Crondell, do you remember me?"

Police Chief Crondell stared at her, recognition dawning in his eyes. "Yes," he responded slowly.

"When we first met, I told you I had a message for the people of Milsap. Do you remember where you sent me?" Leonab asked.

"I believe I sent you to the hospital," replied the curious Police Chief.

"You gave me a map. Do you remember how you described the hospital to me?" Leonab continued, undaunted.

"I told you to go to the white plus sign in the red circle," answered Police Chief Crondell.

Leonab pointed to the cross behind her and said, "I have arrived."

The crowd hushed. The Police Chief said, "It is very unconventional, but under the current circumstances, I think we should hear what the lady has to say."

CHAPTER 25

"What I have to say will be difficult to hear and maybe even harder to believe," began Leonab. "I come to give you a message about the future."

"Oh, a time traveler," shouted someone to her right, and several people on both sides of the room laughed.

"Decisions you make today will affect your people's future as well as the future of my people. Do you not see how your own values are conflicted? Those of you opposed to the murder of innocent children, are you not enabling others to murder those children? Those of you who esteem personal choice of what you do with your own bodies, are you not limiting what other people do with their own money? Those of you who esteem personal choice in who you love, do you not wish to restrict what someone else owns?"

"Why don't we send you further in the past to solve all these contradictions?" taunted someone in the front. "You didn't have to stop here."

"I do not doubt that this inefficient people would try such a thing. Even your prophet Jwo has said, 'You cannot change history, you can only learn from it.' But you misunderstand me, sir. I am not from your future, come to change the past for my sake. I am from the past, sent by the one true God to deliver a message of pending judgment but also to offer hope and peace," Leonab responded to a now silent crowd.

> "This is what the Lord says, 'For three sins of the land of Milsap and for four, I will pour out my judgment upon you and raze your city to the ground because you have exalted self-interest above the interest of others; you have slain the weak and the lame, the blind and the innocent for your own personal convenience. You have made orphans of your very own seed and sacrificed them by your own hand for your own gain. You have valued interpretive psychology over my natural biology. You exalt your reasons, but you have no reason.

> "'To the lampstand that is at Milsap, I have somewhat against you because you have exalted your own rights and ownership over my kingdom. Will you build your own kingdom and protect it? Will you draw your sword rather than submit to drink of the cup I have prepared for you? Why do you seek to protect and promote your institutions that I have prophesied to you are temporal rather than building my kingdom that will see no end?

> "'Come now, and let us reason together,' says the Lord. 'Though your sins are as scarlet, they will be as white as snow.'"

By the time Leonab finished, Stew was onstage with Mr. Gofson and Mayor Anderson. Stew had only heard the very end of Leonab's message, but he could tell that this was the audience it was meant for. All over the sanctuary, people were approaching the front altar, weeping. Lily and Billy were there, accompanied by a smiling Diana. Stew saw her, nodded, and smiled back. The majority of the people were silent and skeptical, and there were many who scoffed and jeered. Others left without saying anything. *You can't save them all*, Leonab thought.

CHAPTER 26

Leonab stepped back from the pulpit and was approached by the Police Chief. "Now I see and believe that you are the messenger of God. I have been praying for God to send us a sign, to call us back to himself. I'm sorry I didn't recognize you; I had no idea that you—that he—would . . . "

"Jesus met Thomas where he was: 'Reach hither thy finger and behold my hands; reach hither thy hand and thrust it into my side, and believe,'" answered Leonab.

"There's one thing I still don't understand, though," said Police Chief Crondell. "You said you're from the past come to change our future. I suppose I can believe that God could send us a prophet from the days of old, but how does our future affect your future since history cannot change?"

"Yahweh sent me because, without this message, in two generations your people of Milsap would have no representation at his throne. 'Thou wast slain, and hast redeemed us to God by thy blood out of every kindred, and tongue, and people, and nation.' My people will worship Yahweh next to your future generations," Leonab said.

As Leonab exited the stage, the Police Chief took charge at the front, dismissing the crowd but inviting those who wished to stay and earnestly consider the challenge brought to them from God Almighty to meet for prayer. That would be the last Leonab would know of them. As she passed Mayor Anderson, the Gofsons, and Stew, she said, "May Yahweh guide you as you seek him." Then she walked off the stage and disappeared.

CHAPTER 27

Leonab found herself in the darkness of her own home, standing in front of her own teevee, though for the darkness of the night around her, she could barely make out its shape. She walked over to where her daughter was asleep and kissed her head. She found her husband lying asleep a little farther away. She lay down. As she lay in the darkness, her heart raced.

Her husband stirred and dreamily asked, "Have you done all that Yala has called you to do?"

She responded, "The servant of the Lord was careful to do all that Yala has commanded."

As she drifted off to sleep, the word of the Lord came to her, saying:

> Daughter of Woman, bind up the scroll of the vision you have seen. It is not for your generation to know these events. Go and share the good news of my enduring faithfulness, for you alone have seen the

details of the fulfillment of my everlasting promise, but these details are hidden from the present generation until they shall come to pass.

Leonab marveled that Yala spoke her own language as if he had written it himself. She responded in English, though, as he was the only one in her time who could understand. "I thank you, Yala, for trusting your handmaid with so important a task. I would know if Milsap will return to you."

The response came in the same language. "It is finished."

AFTERWORD

It is difficult to imagine a work of fiction being so challenging and convicting, even to the author himself. Yet as this story unfolds and the dialogue flows, even the author cannot help but be overcome by the words from the prophet Leonab's mouth. While she assesses secular society's abandon of reason in pursuit of self-fulfillment, she also has harsh words from the Lord for the religious who live in their own white-picket-fence version of Christianity. What is convicting, of course, is not the storyline or even the logical arguments presented. It is the Holy Spirit's work inside readers to challenge whether their worldviews align with God's principles revealed in scripture. As Leonab reads through the scriptures for the first time, the reader gets a glimpse of the Holy Spirit helping her interpret and process the meaning of the prophecies.

This book does not propose practical solutions to static problems but rather philosophical principles to consider in dynamic situations. The prophets in scripture brought messages of judgment accompanied by promises of hope. Leonab is no different. While she indicts secular and religious cultures alike, she promises that God is not done with the people of Milsap. Likewise, whatever our circumstances, we can be sure God is not ready to write off individuals. There is hope for you no matter what mistakes, trials, or temptations you face.

—Jwo

APPENDIX 1
JWO'S BLOG

thePennedKnight*

I'd rather be a pawn on God's chessboard than the king of my own house of cards.

Time Travel

Is time travel possible? The simplest answer is, "Of course, we do it one day at a time, hour-by-hour, minute-by-minute, second-by-second." Obviously, that is not the underlying intention of question, but I believe the answer is still affirmative, though not exactly the way we perceive it in movies with time machines.

Part 1: Backward Traveling

Can we get back to the past or the Past?

To err is human, to regret even more so. Most if not all people have a few things they wish they could go back and change. Is it possible to go back and make better decisions or take back those harsh words one spoke?

There are various theories on how one's memory works in a fashion to visit one's past. In some respects, this approaches a form of time travel. The observer is in some form or fashion 'reliving' those moments in time. With this broad understanding of time travel, any relic such as a photo or family heirloom that brings back those memories should be considered as a portal to the past (no need for a time machine).

---

*ThePennedKnight, http://thepennedknight.blogspot.com/p/time-travel.html.

Imperfections in the Memory

The quandary with this form of time travel is that one's memories are unreliable. They define the past as the observer remembers it. Memory is imperfect, and one's brain rewrites history in accordance with one's own emotions, preconceived worldviews, post-event worldviews, and assumptions. Over time, one's memory of a single event may change[1]. Even ignoring these flaws in one's own memory, one can only remember events in accordance with his/her perspective at the time. In other words, two observers may have witnessed the same event but remember it differently such that when each 'relives' the same event in their own respective memories, they are not reliving the same things.

> [1] A fascinating side note to the changing memory of an individual is that some of these changes are conscious, and others are subconscious. Conscious changes to one's memory occur when one later learns additional facts which explain the cause of the event or the circumstances surrounding the event. Subconscious and/or unconscious changes to the memory are more complex. This is not a study in psychology, however, the author acknowledges that the human mind is a powerful tool allowing the host to recall, rearrange, modify, and even suppress events subconsciously, perhaps to protect the host's emotional well being or psyche.

Implications of these Imperfections

These imperfections in human memory may cause scenarios such as a) a single observer visits different versions of the same historical event at different moments in his/her life or b) multiple observers visit different versions of the same historical event at the same moment in their lives. This phenomenon could be used to validate a multiverse perspective on history. In fact, this is a logical conclusion considering the modern philosophical view that truth is relative to the observer; many versions of history have occurred, and it is left to the observer to define not only perspective but the how and why of the past to determine the implications on the present and future for him/herself.

A more appropriate interpretation of these imperfections is that they validate the clear distinction between history and History as defined in another work [here]*; fundamentally, that history is from the subjective perspective of the observer and is imperfect but knowable, while History is objective from outside all observers and perfect but unknowable to the observers[2]. This leads to a distinction between the 'past' and the 'Past'.

> [2] These definitions in the context of the original work are based on the assumption that there is no Deity (or Supreme Being), and the only observers addressed are human beings. In this work, the author includes the notion of an all-knowing Deity, and thus, History is known to this Supreme Being.

The past could be defined as a given observer's memory of historical events he/she has witnessed at a specific point in time of the observer's life; this term specifically entails the observer's original perspective on the events (considering the limited extent of the observer's point of view and the observer's worldview and understanding of the situation at the time of occurrence) as well as

* *ThePennedKnight*, http://thepennedknight.blogspot.com/p/a-philosophical treatise-on-odds-and.html.

the conscious and subconscious alterations made to the memory of the events up to the moment of recollection. This past is finite, imperfect, ever changing, and knowable only to the observer, and it ultimately dies with the observer. While an observer can "pass along" memories to another observer, this conveyance is imperfect, and the passed memory becomes convolved into the other observer's past.

The Past could be defined as that portion of History that has occurred in a given individual's life, regardless of the observer's perspective on, relation to, or interpretation of the events themselves. The Past is perfect and unknowable. Using these definitions, some would argue that if several witnesses to a single event were gathered to provide their own detailed accounts of the event from their pasts, that the actual event from the Past could be reconstructed. The author agrees in theory; a mathematical equation could be derived from empirical evidences to quantify the incremental volume of information provided by each witness to the composite account of the event and identify the maximum number of witnesses necessary to provide all knowable details[3]. The issue with generating such an equation and with the concept of deconvolving the Past from various pasts is that it is based on the presumption that a) each facet of the Past must necessarily have been observed by at least one observer such that all facets were observed by the sum of the witnesses, b) each individual observer would completely and honestly relate his/her observations, and c) an independent individual compiling the various components from all of the pasts could accurately distinguish between factual observations and interpretive/revisionist observations. The author believes these are impossible and therefore agrees in theory but does not agree that it could be brought to practice.

(3) While this discussion addresses the philosophical entirety of the Past, the author recognizes that materiality is of primary import in the vast majority of situations, while the precise details may be less critical. For most events in which immediate judgment or assignation of culpability is required, one or two witnesses are sufficient to provide an adequate assessment of a situation. In a traffic accident, for instance, the color of the cell phone being used to text while driving, while being of philosophical import to the precise account of the Past, is immaterial to the specific question of whether or not one is at fault. Therefore, if two witnesses disagree on the color of the cell phone but agree that the same driver was texting while driving, this information may be sufficient to determine the cause of the accident.

Imprecise Visits to the Past

Having defined these two related but distinct terms, we return to the concept of traveling to the past or Past. Since the past is the observer's version of the Past, when an individual relives a specific event, he/she is only visiting a possible historical event. Since time traveling must necessarily involve reliving the Past (or precisely viewing the unknowable, perfect, Historical event), reliving a memory should be considered relative time travel (perhaps we should expand Einstein's general theory of relativity).

What if, like Ebenezer Scrooge, one were to be visited by the Ghost of the Past? As long as this Ghost of the Past contains the qualities ascribed to the all-knowing Deity, then time travel with this Entity would be perfectly possible.

Can we travel back in history or History?

It was important to begin with a specific individual observer's memory before broaching the more general subject matter of time travel through history or History. Now that we have laid the groundwork for the differences between the past and Past, let us further clarify that history considers the human account of History. In other words, while the past is a set of memories over a given observer's lifetime, history is the account of all known observations of events by humans since records have been kept. Once again, history is incomplete and must rely on deductive and inductive reasoning to supplement human understanding of the perfect but unknowable History.

Now is it possible to travel back in History? There are two distinct periods of History, a) pre-human observer and b) post-human observer, or more precisely pre- and post-human recorded observations. Let's first discuss the latter because it is the most similar to our discussion on the past versus the Past. An observer could certainly conceptualize or 'relive' someone else's account of Historical events even if that original observer were no longer alive to verbally describe or recreate said events personally. In that regard, the living observer is able to travel with the original observer through his/her own past. However, as we've already indicated, one observer is not only limited in perspective but also in worldview, and memory is subject to conscious and subconscious biases that the new observer will not be able to deconvolve. Could an Historical event be recreated from several original observers? This is yet again impossible because of the upper limit on viewpoints, complete honesty, and observer biases[4]. So this discourse returns to the potential multiverse of potential histories just over the observed and recorded time period.

[4] Again, in this case, materiality is of utmost import. For instance, if several people lived through the St. Mary Magdalene's flood in the 1300s, and presented

verbal testimony of the event afterward, while the precise amount of rainfall (part of History) is unattainable, the lack of this information does not negate the Historicity of the event itself. An event can be Historical without humanity having the precise History of the event. While an observer would not be able to revisit the Historical event (proper time travel), he/she could relive interpretations of the event from history, which is consistent with relative time travel.

When considering time travel to a point pre-human recorded observations, there is an even broader disconnect since all of our understanding of that point in History has been gathered with deductive and inductive reasoning projecting backward from what has been observed to a time when no observer or recorder was present. This backward projection is a non-unique solution, and in fact, there are various versions of history prior to human records[5]. Therefore, in addition to one's own limited perspective in one's own imprecise, ever-changing memory, in addition to the inaccurate, convoluted, and biased memories of others, an observer is now faced with a variety of interpretations of these observed and recorded events and their projections backward through time to these histories (not Histories). In this event, it is much simpler to acknowledge that travel to History is impossible, though it is still not impossible to identify Historical events and relive historical versions of these.

[5] Here it is significant to note that just as an observer has a specific point of view in his/her own memory, one's perspective or worldview may also affect his or her projection through historical records to a bias.

Could one be visited by the Ghost of History? As long as this Deity exists, it is plausible that He/She could in fact visit an observer and escort him/her through History. The notion is somewhat mute, however, since any observer could merely claim to have been visited by the Deity, and others would have little to no recourse to test the veracity of the claim. Unless the Deity determines to visit all observers, such time travel is nearly meaningless because it cannot be conclusive.

Subconscious Backward Time Travel

In general, the foregoing discussion has addressed intentional strolls down memory lane. But there are situations in which individuals subconsciously get stuck in reliving past failures or victories. Neither of these tendencies to live in the past is healthy. One who relives his/her past failures continues to grieve over and over again for mistakes that cannot be undone. One who constantly relives his/her past successes is blinded by self love. In traveling to the past, one cannot change the events thereof nor bring them forward to the present. There are others who suffer from haunting, suppressed memories. Each of these cases causes an individual to lose sight of the present and miss out on opportunities to build or repair relationships and grow personally.

Conclusion of Part 1

Is it possible to travel backward in time? The answer is a resounding somewhat. Ultimately, an individual can use relative time travel to:

a. relive one's own imperfect memories.
b. visit someone else's memories.
c. review collective, imprecise accounts of Historical events.

d. recreate illustrations of Historical events pre-human recorded observations.

e. conceive projections of theoretical historical events.

With this understanding, mental time travel is possible, but
revisiting these events cannot be conclusive to define History in
its entirety, however, histories of single Historical events can be
relived for the purposes of substantiation and education.

Part 2: Forward Traveling

Can we get to the future or Future?

Einstein's theory of relativity gives a specific illustration of how
we can travel to the future by traveling at high speeds. In fact,
this has been demonstrated through experiments in which
2 identical atomic clocks are synchronized, and then one is
placed in an airplane flying around the earth while the other sits
motionless on the ground. The clock in motion runs slower than
the stationary clock, and therefore travels forward in time. If an
individual could travel at speeds approaching the speed of light,
he/she could travel farther than a few seconds or minutes into the
future. Time machines and wormholes remain to be proven, but
nonexistence at present does not preclude future existence.

Future Possibilities

Obviously, no one has memories of the future, but similar to an
individual's past he/she has visions or expectations of the future
that affect how he/she behaves in the present. For instance,
anyone who invests in a retirement account of any kind is
envisioning a future time when he/she is no longer working full
time. Purchasing life insurance and investing in a retirement
account at the same time is like planning for the multiverse of

potential futures. We don't call this time travel, we call this being financially responsible.

Future time travel is not solely associated with financial decisions. On a daily basis, many people have a tendency to worry about a possible future event. In these situations, an individual is envisioning some negative future occurrence and travels to the potential future mentally and projects anxiety back onto the present. In general, remembering a more recent historical event is easier than remembering an older event. The same is true for the future; humans are better at predicting and planning for the near-term future than for the long-term future. Planning for breakfast tomorrow morning is easier and more practical than preparing for retirement. The near-term future is more concrete than long-term future.

The author is hesitant to differentiate the future from the Future. The author does not wish to imply that the Future is established as History is, however, it is convenient to distinguish an individual's projections of potential future events versus what actually will happen in the Future.

Events of the Future are similar to Historical events in that an individual may know that some event has occurred in History or an event will occur in the Future, but the precise details cannot be fully comprehended. For instance, each individual was born in his/her own past, yet the details cannot be fully known in the Past; and each individual will someday die in their future[6] though we cannot be certain of the time, place, or circumstances in the Future. As Benjamin Franklin said, "There are only 2 things certain in life, death and taxes."*

---

*Benjamin Franklin, quoted in "Death and Taxes," Adam Smith Institute, https://www.adamsmith.org/blog/death-and-taxes.

(6) The author acknowledges that events such as one's death are generally spoken of in terms of the subjunctive to convey the uncertainty of it. If the reader wishes to take exception to this assumption, the author suggests reviewing 1) the underwhelming statistics of persons born who have not died and 2) the Biblical passage, Hebrews 9:27, " . . . it is appointed for people to die once-and after this, judgement" (CSB).

Could one be visited by the Ghost of the Future? As long as the Deity exists, it is plausible that He/She could in fact visit an observer and escort him/her through the Future. In fact, some have claimed to have viewed the Future and made predictions. Some of these would-be prophets predict far-off events making it impossible to validate the predictions during his/her lifetime, but for those who predict events in the near-term, either the forecasts bear out or they do not.

Forward Looking Statements

Government regulation requires publicly traded companies to warn investors about the uncertainty of the future with disclaimers such as, "This presentation contains forward-looking statements, including forecasts of future revenue, profits, and expenses related to expected business events. Such statements are subject to risk, uncertainties, and other factors, some of which are beyond the control of [presenter], which may cause actual results to vary materially from those expressed in forward-looking statements."

Why are disclaimers like this required? Isn't it obvious that no one can accurately predict the future? Well, these disclaimers are designed to clarify the risk and uncertainty surrounding the projections. Risk and uncertainty are sometimes used synonymously, however, there is a very clear difference between the two words. In simple terms, risk is used to address chance of success or failure, while uncertainty addresses a range of potential successful outcomes. An investor takes a risk by investing in a new widget-making company that has no sales contracts and is not currently producing any widgets; the primary question is of success or failure. An investor faces uncertainty when purchasing stock in an existing widget-making company who is currently selling X widgets per month with potential to sell 2X widgets per month; the primary question is on the range of success. There are many possible future outcomes, each with associated risk and/or uncertainty.

If an individual would assess the risk and uncertainty associated with dreaded future events, perhaps he/she would be less prone to assume the worst possible outcome, which results in constant worry.

Subconscious Forward Time Travel

In general, the foregoing discussion has addressed conscious views into potential futures to adjust current behavior. But, there are situations in which individuals subconsciously travel to potential negative futures resulting in anxiety and dread or travel to potential positive futures and live in daydreams. These cases are the most difficult to correct since logic cannot be employed to reason with the subconscious. In these cases, the author suggests that each individual struggling with this type of subconscious habit take stock of their circumstance during a period of calm. It is in this period of calm where the individual can reason with themselves considering following:

    a.   The subconscious mind is a prophet of future doom or bloom.

    b.   These prophecies lead to recurring anxiety or fancy.

c. How often do these predictions come to fruition?

d. How good of a prophet is the subconscious mind?

One can then prepare for the next anxiety attack or daydream by devising a plan to remind him/her self of these facts. Each individual is different, and for some medication or other exterior support may be required.

Conclusion of Part 2
Is it possible to travel forward in time? The answer is a resounding somewhat. Ultimately, an individual can imagine many potential future outcomes, and while certain events of the Future can be expected, timing and circumstances cannot be completely defined. Anytime an individual alters his/her current behavior in anticipation of some future event, he/she has, to some extent, traveled to the future mentally.

Part 3: Living in the Present
The year was 1985 when Marty McFly traveled to the past in the DeLorean with the help of Doc Brown and a little plutonium. Marty, a high school student went back to meet his parents during their high school years and wound up changing his present-day life by setting up his parents' union in a spectacular way. The name of the film was, of course, "Back to the Future." The movie communicates an interesting but clear message that an individual's past affects his/her present and future[7].

[7] The whole notion of backward and forward time travel suggests a linear view of time, which has been considered by many scientists and philosophers alike. Some would suggest that time is circular, a notion that may be supported by the fact that history seems

to repeat itself or perhaps even on a simpler level, by instances of déjà vu. The author believes this is an example of the unknowable and therefore chooses to employ Occam's Razor, electing the linear view of time as the simplest explanation.

The Present is the Future

Today is yesterday's tomorrow. Many people tell themselves that they will begin dieting or changing some habit in the future when in fact, they have been preparing for today for all of their lives. Consider the account of David and Goliath. While the soldiers of Israel's army are shaking in their boots at Goliath's challenge, David approaches King Saul and says, 'I'll defeat the giant'. At the king's expression of his doubts, David travels back to his past to relate his experiences when God delivered him from the lion and the bear, and based on those historical experiences, David has faith that God will deliver in the future. Because David was faithful in each of these moments, not waiting for some grandiose opportunity to trust God, he is prepared for the battle with the giant.

The Present Is the Past

Today is tomorrow's yesterday. In reality, whatever one wishes to be able to accomplish tomorrow, one must begin doing today. We become what we prepare to be. Consider Hebrews 12:2, " . . . Jesus . . . for the joy that lay before him, endured the cross . . . " (CSB). Jesus knew that He was living in the past and was able to travel to the future and project the future joy back to the present, so He was able to endure the cross. Whatever one does today will determine what opportunities he/she has tomorrow and will define who he/she is tomorrow.

APPENDIX 2
ONE MORE GOODBYE

Verse 1a

    (There was a) time when all the world was right

    (When) love and music filled my life

    (The) flowers bloomed and birds would sing

    (And) spring was into everything

Verse 1b

    (Now) I've returned to normalcy

    (My) life is mediocrity

    Since she left me all alone

    (And I) can't determine what went wrong

Chorus 1

    When I see her face on someone new

    I think about the way that our love grew

    (And) tears start forming in my eyes

    (As) heartbreak sets in one more time

Verse 2a

    (Some say) loneliness and solitude

    (Are) all that we look forward to

    (But) speaking from my emptiness

    (I) can't believe that dreariness

Verse 2b

(The) poets tell of joy and tears
(Of) sorrows, pain, surprise, and fears
(But) who can say that this is real
(And) who can tell me what to feel

Chorus 2

('Cause) when I see her face on someone new
I think about the way that our love grew
(And) tears start forming in my eyes
(As) heartbreak sets in one more time

Verse 3a

(Can you) tell me how to say goodbye
(And) how to hold my head up high
(Does) heartbreak heal with Tylenol
(Or) does it ever heal at all

Verse 3b

(They) say it's just psychology
(And) love is just philosophy
(She's) passed into another land
(So I) should find peace and understand

Chorus 3

(But) when I see her face on someone new
(I) think about the way that our love grew
(And) tears start forming in my eyes
(As) heartbreak sets in one more time

Bridge

(I) think about the years as they've gone by

(And I) hang my head and fight the urge to cry

(As) grief turns into apathy

(I) wonder when I will be free

Final Chorus

Then I see her face on someone else

(And I) start to feel sorry for myself

(And) tears start forming in my eyes

(As) heartbreak sets in one more time

www.ingramcontent.com/pod-product-compliance
Lightning Source LLC
Chambersburg PA
CBHW071444090426
42737CB00011B/1766